Ac

A Selection of Passages
from the Teachings of
J. Krishnamurti

Krishnamurti Publications of America

Action

A Selection of Passages
from the Teachings of
J. Krishnamurti

©1990 by the Krishnamurti Foundation of America

Revised edition, 2000

Editor: Albion W. Patterson

ISBN 1-888004-01-0

Publisher: Krishnamurti Publications of America
For information and a complete catalogue of Krishnamurti
books, videotapes, and audiotapes write:

Krishnamurti Foundation of America
P.O. Box 1560, Ojai, California 93024
U.S.A.
www.kfa.org

10 9 8 7 6 5 4 3

Contents

Foreword

The passages in this Study Book have been taken directly from Krishnamurti's talks and books from 1933 through 1967. The compilers began by reading all the passages from this period which contained the word *action*—the theme of this book. This would not have been possible without the use of a full text computer database, produced by the Krishnamurti Foundation Trust of England. Over 750 passages were studied in all, and the aspects of "action" most frequently addressed by Krishnamurti were noted. These aspects then formed the outline for the contents of this book.

The material selected has not been altered from the way it was originally printed except for limited correction of spelling, punctuation, and missing words. Words or phrases that appear in brackets are not Krishnamurti's, but have been added by the compilers for the sake of clarity. Ellipses introducing a passage, or ending it, indicate that the passage begins or ends in mid-sentence. Ellipses in the course of a passage indicate words or sentences omitted. A series of asterisks between paragraphs shows that there are paragraphs from that talk which have been omitted. Captions, set off from the body of the text, have been used with many passages. Most captions are statements taken directly from the text, with some being a combination of phrases from the passage.

Krishnamurti spoke from such a large perspective that his entire vision was implied in any extended passage. If one wishes to see how a statement flows out of his whole discourse, one can find the full context from the references at the foot of each passage. These refer primarily to talks which have been published in *The Collected Works of J. Krishnamurti*. This seventeen-volume set covers the entire period from which this study book has been drawn. A complete bibliography is included at the end of this book. Students and scholars may also be interested in additional passages on action not used in the book, available for study upon written request, in the archives of the Krishnamurti Foundation of America.

This Study Book aims to give the reader as comprehensive a view as possible, in 140 pages, of the question of action as explored by Krishnamurti during the period covered. Most of the material presented has not been previously published, except in the Verbatim Reports which were produced privately, in limited numbers, primarily for those who attended Krishnamurti's talks.

A final note: The term *heuristic*, used in the heading of section VI, is defined by the *Chambers Twentieth Century Dictionary*[1] as "serving or leading to find out" or "the method in education by which the pupil is set to find out things for himself" and <u>not</u> "depending on assumptions based on past experience."

Albion W. Patterson, Editor

[1] *Chambers Twentieth Century Dictionary,* New Edition, Edinburgh, Chambers, 1972, p. 612

Introduction

Talking things over together as two friends...

In a few days we are going to have discussions, and we can start those discussions this morning. But if you assert and I assert, if you stick to your opinion, to your dogma, to your experience, to your knowledge, and I stick to mine, then there can be no real discussion because neither of us is free to inquire. To discuss is not to share our experiences with each other. There is no sharing at all; there is only the beauty of truth, which neither you nor I can possess. It is simply there.

To discuss intelligently, there must also be a quality not only of affection but of hesitation. You know, unless you hesitate, you can't inquire. Inquiry means hesitating, finding out for yourself, discovering step by step; and when you do that, then you need not follow anybody, you need not ask for correction or for confirmation of your discovery. But all this demands a great deal of intelligence and sensitivity.

By saying that, I hope I have not stopped you from asking questions! You know, this is like talking things over together as two friends. We are neither asserting nor seeking to dominate each other, but each is talking easily, affably, in an atmosphere of friendly companionship, trying to discover. And in that state of mind we do discover, but I assure you, what we discover has very little importance. The important thing is to discover, and after discovering, to keep going. It is detrimental to stay with what you have discovered, for then your mind is closed, finished. But if you die to what you have discovered the moment you have discovered it, then you can flow like the stream, like a river that has an abundance of water.

Saanen, 10th Public Talk, August 1, 1965
Collected Works, Vol. XV, p. 245

3

I.
An Overview

In learning there is no end and that is the beauty...the sacredness of life.

So you and I will go into this together. You are not going to learn anything from me, you are not going to gather something here and go away with it, because if you do that, it will be merely an accumulation, something which you store up to remember. But as I am talking, please listen with your whole being, with your full attention, with eagerness, as you would listen to something which you really love—if you ever do love. Because here you are receiving no instructions and you are not a pupil. You are learning an art—and I really do mean that. We are learning together and therefore the division of the teacher and the disciple has completely gone. It is immature thinking to regard somebody as a teacher who knows and yourself as one who does not know. In that relationship both lack humility and therefore both cease to learn. This is not just a verbal expression, a temporary statement, as you will see for yourself if you listen without merely looking for instructions as to what to do and what not to do. Life is not understood through a series of instructions. You can apply instructions to a dynamo, the radio, but life is not a machine, it is an ever-living, ever-renewing thing. So, there is no instruction—and that is the beauty of learning. The mind that is small, instructed, taught, only strengthens memory—as happens in all the universities and schools where you merely cultivate memory in order to pass examinations and get a job. That is not acquiring intelligence. Intelligence comes when you are learning. In learning there is no end, and that is the beauty of life, the sacredness of life. So you and I are going to learn, to explore, think together and communicate with each other about action.

To most of us life is action, and by action we mean something which has been done, is being done, or will be done. Without action you cannot live. Action does not mean only physical movement, going from here to there; there is also the action of thought, the action of an idea, the action of a feeling, of environment, of opinion, the action of ambition, of food and of psychological influences—of which most of us are totally unaware. There are the actions of the conscious mind and the actions of the unconscious mind. There is also, is there not, the action of a seed in the earth, the action of a man who gets a job and sticks to it for the rest of his life; there is the action of the waves beating on the shore, the action of gentle weather, of rain; there is all the action of the earth and of the heavens. So action is something limitless. Action is a movement both within and out of time. I am thinking aloud with you; I am exploring. I came here with one thought, action, and I want to discuss it with you, go into it, explore it gently, slowly, quietly, so that you and I understand it together.

But when you merely reduce action to: "What am I to do? Should I do this and not do that? Is this right, or that?" then action becomes a very small thing. We do, naturally, have to act within time; I do have to stop at the end of the hour; one has to go to the office, the factory, take meals, at a certain time. There must be action in time, and that is all we know, is it not? You and I really do not know anything else except action which is recognizable and within the field of time. By time we mean yesterday, today, and tomorrow. Tomorrow is the infinite future, yesterday is the infinite past, and today is the present; and the conflict between the future and the past produces a thing which we call action. So we are always inquiring how to act within the field of time, of recognition. We are always asking what to do: whether to marry or not to marry, whether to yield to temptation or to resist, whether to try and become rich or seek God. Circumstances—which are really the same as time—force me to accept a job because I have a family and I have to earn, and so there is all the conflict, turmoil and toil. So my mind is caught in the field of action-within-time. That is all I know; and each action produces its own result, its own fruits, again within time. That is one step, is it not? To see that we are caught in the action of time.

Then there is the action of tension. Please follow this, because we are examining it together. There is the action born of the tension between two opposites, which is a state of self-contradiction— wanting to do this and doing totally the opposite. You know that, do you not? One desire says, do this and another desire says, do not do it. You are feeling angry, violent, brutal, and yet a part of you tells you to be kind, to be gentle, nice. For most of us action is born out of tension, self-contradiction. If you watch yourself you will see it; and the more the struggle, the contradiction, the more drastic and violent is the action. Out of this tension the ambitious man works ruthlessly—in the name of God, in the name of peace, or in the name of politics, of his country, and so on. Such tension produces great action; and the man who is in an agony of self-contradiction may produce a poem, a book, a painting; the greater the inward tension the greater the activity, the productivity.

Then, if you will observe in yourself, there is also the action of will. I must do this and I must not do that. I must discipline myself. I must not think this way. I must reject, I must protect. So there is the positive and the negative action of will. I am just describing and, if you are really listening, you will see that an action of real understanding takes place—which I am going to go through presently. The action of will is the action of resistance, negatively or positively. So there are varieties of action, but most of us know the action of will because most of us have no great tension since we are not great. We are not great writers, great politicians or great saints, so-called; they are not really saints at all because they have committed themselves to a certain form of life and therefore have ceased to learn. We are ordinary people, not too clever. Sometimes we look at a tree or a sunset and smile happily, but for most of us action is born of will; we are resisting. Will is the result of many desires, is it not? You know, do you not, the action of will—I feel lazy and I would like to lie in bed a little longer but I must discipline myself and get up; I feel sexual, lustful, but I must not, I must resist it. So we exercise will to produce a result. That is all we know; either we yield or resist, and yielding creates its own agony which presently becomes resistance. So we are everlastingly in battle within ourselves.

So, will is the product of desire, wanting and not wanting. It is as simple as that, do not let us complicate it—leave that to the philosophers, the speculators. You and I know that will is the action that is born within the field of two opposite desires, and our cultivation of virtue is the cultivation of resistance. Resisting envy you call virtuous. And that is going on always within us—a desire producing its opposite and from the opposite a resistance is created, and that resistance is will. If you watch your own mind you will see it. And as we have to move in this world we exercise this will, and that is all we know, and with this will we say we must find out if there is something beyond. With this will we discipline ourselves, torture ourselves, deny ourselves—and the more you are capable of denying yourself the more saintly you are supposed to be. All your saints, your gurus and gods are the product of this denial, this resistance; and the man who can follow ardently, denying everything, following the ideal he has projected, him you call a great man.

So when you look at this life of action—the growing tree, the bird on the wing, the flowing river, the movement of the clouds, of lightning, of machines, the action of the waves upon the shore—then you see, do you not, that life itself is action, endless action that has no beginning and no end. It is something that is everlastingly in movement, and it is the universe, God, bliss, reality. But we reduce the vast action of life to our own petty little action in life, and ask what we should do, or follow some book, some system. See what we have done, how petty, small, narrow, ugly, brutal our action is. Please do listen to this! I know as well as you that we have to live in this world, that we have to act within time and that it is no good saying: "Life is so vast, I will let it act, it will tell me what to do." It won't tell us what to do. So you and I have to see this extraordinary phenomenon of our mind reducing this action which is infinite, limitless, profound, to the pettiness of how to get a job, how to become a minister, whether to have sex or not—you know all the petty little struggles in life. So we are constantly reducing this enormous movement of life to action which is recognizable and made respectable by society. You see this, sirs, do you not—the action which is recognizable and within the field of time, and that action which knows no recognition and which is the endless movement of life.

Now, the question is this: Can I live in this world, do my job and so on, with a sense of this endless depth of action, or must I, through my petty mind, reduce action to a functioning only within the field of recognition, within the field of time? Am I making myself clear?

Let me put the thing differently. Love is something which is not measurable in terms of action, is it not? I do not know if you have ever thought about it. You and I are talking together now face to face and we are both interested in this and want to find out. We know what this feeling of beauty, of love is. We are talking of love itself, not the explanation of love, not the verbal expression. The word *love* is not love. Though the intellectual mind divides it into profane love and sacred, divine love, all that has no meaning. But that beauty of feeling which is not expressible in words and not recognizable by the mind—we know that thing. It is really a most extraordinary thing; in it there is no sense of 'the other', and the observer is absent; there is only the feeling. It is not that I feel love and express it by holding your hand or by doing this or that act. It *is*. If you have ever had that feeling, if you have ever lived it, if you have understood it, expressed it, nurtured it, if you have felt it totally with all your being, you will see that with that feeling one can live in the world. Then you can educate your children in the most splendid manner, because that feeling is the center of action, though within the field of time. But not having that feeling, with all its immensity, passion, and vigor, we reduce love merely to the "I love you" and function only within the field of time, trying to catch the eye of another.

So you see the problem. Love is something that knows no measure, that cannot be put together by the mind, cannot be cultivated, something which is not sentimental, which has nothing to do with emotionalism and nothing whatsoever to do with good works—the village reform and so on. When you have that feeling then everything in life is important, significant; therefore you will do that which is good. But without knowing the beauty, the depth, the vigour of it we are trying to reduce love into something which the mind can capture and make respectable. And the same applies to action, which we are now trying to understand.

Action is an endless movement which has no beginning and no end and which is not controlled by cause and effect. Action is of everything—the action of the sea, of the mango seed becoming the mango tree, and so on. But the human mind is not a seed and therefore, through its action it becomes only a modified reproduction of what it was. In our life there is the constant pressure of circumstances, and although the circumstances are always changing, they are ever shaping our lives. What was, is not; what is, can be broken. So can we not sense, feel, this enormous action of life which ranges from the movement of the little worm in the earth to the sweep of the infinite heavens? If you really want to know what this extraordinary thing is, this action, then you must go through it, you must break through the barrier of this action in time. Then you will know it, then with that feeling you can act, you can go to your job and do all the things that are recognizable within the field of time. But from within the recognizable field of time you cannot find the other. Do what you will, through the petty you will never find the immeasurable.

If you once really saw the truth of this—that a mind functioning within the field of time can never understand the eternal, which is outside of time—if you really saw that, felt it, then you would see that a mind which speculates about love and divides it up as carnal, profane, divine or sacred can never find the other. But if you can feel this astonishing action—the movement of the stars, the forests, the rivers, the ocean, the ways of the animals and of human beings—if you could know the beauty of a tender leaf in spring, the feeling of rain as it drops from the heavens, then with that immense feeling you can act within the field of recognition, within the field of time. But action within the field of time can never lead to the other. If you really understand that, not verbally, intellectually, if you really feel the significance of it, grasp it, see the extraordinary beauty and loveliness of it, then you will see that the will has no place in this at all. All action born of will is essentially self-centered, egocentric, but such action will disappear totally when you have understood it fully, when you have really felt yourself moving in it, with your mind wholly in it. Then you can see that there is no necessity for will at all; there is a quite different movement. The will then is like a knotted piece of rope, it can be undone. That will can be lost; but the other cannot be lost, it cannot be increased or decreased.

So, if you are listening with your whole being, learning with your whole being, which means feeling deeply, not merely listening to words intellectually, then you will feel the extraordinary movement of learning, of God—not the god made by the hand or by the mind, not the god of the temple, mosque or church, but this endless immeasurable thing, the timeless. Then you will see that we can live with astonishing peace in this world; then there is no such thing as temptation, no such thing as virtue, because virtue is merely a thing of society. The man who understands all this, who lives it, is orderly, inwardly at rest; his action is entirely different, much more effective, easier and clearer, because there is no inward confusion, contradiction.

So, a mind that holds to conclusions is never humble. A man who has learned is carrying the burden of his knowledge, but a man who is learning has no burden and therefore he can go to the top of the mountain. As two human beings, you and I have talked of something which cannot be captured through words; but by listening to each other, exploring it, understanding it, we have found something extraordinary, something that is imperishable. Life reduced to the 'me' clinging to life is perishable, but if you can see that extraordinary life from the beginning to the end, if once you have gone into it, felt it, drunk at its fountain, then you can live an ordinary life with utter newness, you can really live. The respectable man is not living, he is already dead; and life is not a thing to be invited by the dead. Life is to be entered and forgotten—because there is no 'me' to remember the living of that life. It is only when the mind is in a state of complete humility, when it has no purpose for its own little existence, when it does not move from a point to a point, from experience to experience, from knowledge to knowledge—only such a mind which is totally, completely, wholly not-seeking knows the infinite beginning and the infinite end of existence.

Bombay, 2nd Public Talk, November 30, 1958
Collected Works, Vol. XI, pp. 109-13

II.
What is Action?

Our life is action: going to the market, cooking, breeding children, thinking, going for a drive, looking at a tree, going to the office. All life is tremendous action. If you sit quietly in a forest in springtime, you see that everything is burstingly alive. You know, most of us never die, and therefore we never produce. The trees bring forth new leaves, and when the leaves die they are marvelous to look at. But we live on in the past, we never die, and therefore we never renew, our action is always imitative, conforming, following the pattern of pleasure, and hence there is agony.

Paris, 3rd Public Talk, May 23, 1965
Collected Works, Vol. XV, p. 168

Life—the totality of life—...is action.

We are talking this evening about the question of action. But to understand it, not merely verbally, not merely intellectually, but with a totality of one's whole being, one has to go beyond words. It is only then there is communion, there is sharing, there is partaking together of something vital. And this question of action needs not only a verbal explanation, but rather, and much more, a moving together, feeling our way hesitantly together, into this question of what is action.

* * * * *

Life is existence, is a movement, and this movement is action. Life—the totality of life, not parts of it, the whole state of existence—is action. But when we merely exist, as most of us do, then the problem of action becomes complex. Existence has no division. It is not a fragmentary state of mind or being; in that [state] a totality of action is possible. But when we divide existence into different segments, fragments, then action becomes contradictory.

Bombay, 3rd Public Talk, February 17, 1965
Collected Works, Vol. XV, p. 62

Life is action from the beginning to the end...

I do not know if you have noticed in the morning, high up in the sky, the big vultures, the big birds, flying without a movement of their wings, flying by the current of the air, silently moving. That is action. And also the worm under the earth, eating—that too is activity, that is also action. So also is it action when a politician gets up on the platform and says nothing, or when a person writes, reads, or makes a statue out of marble. That is also action when a man, who has a family, goes to the office for the next forty years, day after day, doing drudgery work without much meaning, wasting his life endlessly about nothing! All that a scientist, an artist, a musician, a speaker does—that too is action. Life is action from the beginning to the end; the whole movement is action.

Rajghat, Banaras, 3rd Public Talk, November 28, 1965
Collected Works, Vol. XV, p. 344

Life is all relationship...action and relationship are synonymous.

We are dealing with action at all the levels of our being—not only the physical act, but the emotional, the psychological, the mental, the unconscious, the conscious act—because that is life. Life is all relationship or action. You cannot escape from these two facts, though action and relationship are synonymous. By "action" we mean that which was done, and that which has to be done, and that which is going to be done. It is a movement, either a continuous movement or a disjointed movement. With most of us, it is disjointed. We live at different levels; there is the office, there is the family, there is public opinion; there are my fears and my gods, my opinions, my judgments, my conditioning; and there are the various pressures, influences of society and so on. We live at different levels, disjointed, unrelated with each other.

Rajghat, Banaras, 3rd Public Talk, December 8, 1963
Collected Works, Vol. XIV, p. 68

Right action comes in understanding relationship...

So relationship is our problem, and without understanding relationship, merely to be active is to produce further confusion, further misery. Action is relationship: to be is to be related. Do what you will—withdraw to the mountains, sit in a forest—you cannot live in isolation. You can live only in relationship, and as long as relationship is not understood, there can be no right action. Right action comes in understanding relationship, which reveals the process of oneself. Self-knowledge is the beginning of wisdom; it is a field of affection, warmth, and love, therefore a field rich with flowers.

Poona, India, 4th Public Talk, September 19, 1948
Collected Works, Vol. V, pp. 96-7

How does one come to discover...an action that is total, whole, not partial?

Unfortunately, we have divided action into fragments: noble action, ignoble action, political action, religious action, scientific action, the action of the reformer, the action of the socialist, the action of the communist, and so on and on. We have broken it up, and therefore there is a contradiction between each action, and there is no understanding of the total movement of action.

And in our own lives, the activity in your house is not so very different from the activity in your office. You are equally ambitious in the office as you are at home. At home, you dominate, oppress, nag, drive—sexually and in so many different ways. Also you are doing the same outside the home. There is the action of a mind that seeks peace, that says, "I must find truth." Such a mind is also in action.

Now, maturity is the comprehension of action as a whole, not as fragments. I am not defining maturity, so do not learn the definition by heart, or learn another definition. You can see that as long as action is fragmentary, there must be contradiction and therefore conflict.

So how does one come to discover or to feel or to live in the active present, in an action that is total, whole, not partial? Have I made my question clear? We have to understand this question because our actions are fragmentary—the religious, the business, the political, the family, and so on; each is different, at least in our minds. And so the worldly man says, "I cannot be religious because I have to earn a livelihood." And the religious man says, "You must leave the world to find God." So everything, every action, is in contradiction. And therefore out of that contradiction there is effort, and in that contradiction there is sorrow, fear, misery, and all the rest of it.

So is there an action which is total so that it has no fragmentation as action, which is life, total life? Unless one understands that, all our actions will be in contradiction. So how does one learn about it? Not "having learned" or "going to learn" but actually "learning" about action which is total, which is not fragmentary. Right? I have put the question. If the problem is clear, we can go on.

Rajghat, Banaras, 3rd Public Talk, November 28, 1965
Collected Works, Vol. XV, pp. 344-5

Krishnamurti: …How am I to put an end to conflict in action?

Questioner: Don't act.

Krishnamurti: My life is action. Talking is action; breathing is action; to see something is an action; to get into a car, to go to my house is action. Everything I do is action. You tell me, "Don't act"! Does that mean just to stop where I am, not think, not feel; to be paralyzed, to be dead?

Questioner: The idea, which is unreal, and reality can never go together.

Krishnamurti: I realize that action is life. Unless I am totally paralyzed, dead or insensitive, I must act. I see that every action breeds more pain, more conflict, more travail. I am going to find out if there is an action in which there is no conflict.

Saanen, 3rd Public Dialogue, August 5, 1966
Collected Works, Vol. XVI, p. 271

III.
Total Action vs. Incomplete Action

Is it possible to see the truth of something immediately, instantly, and act instantly on that which is seen...?

For most of us action is divided. There is a gap between idea and action. We have the formula, the pattern, the concept, the prototype; and according to that we act or approximate our action to that idea. That is our conditioning, that is the way we live—that is, the whole series of our actions is based on that. First we conceive, formulate, create a prototype, the ideal, the thing that should be; and then according to that we live, we act. And thereby our problem is: how to bridge the gap between the action and the idea, how to bring the two together? And in that, there is conflict; in that, there is duration of time, because we need time to complete the action according to the idea.

So what I want to say this evening is that the mind that gives root to a problem ceases to act, because action is always in the living present, in the active present. When the problem becomes something to be solved eventually, then the idea becomes important, not the action.

Please, this is very important to understand because of what I am going to say presently. I have not prepared the talk. I am thinking aloud, and you have also to think within yourself aloud, think of your own processes, be aware of them so that we can go together.

For me there is no action if it is preceded by an idea. If action is conditioned by an idea, by a formula, by a concept, action then is not important but the idea is important, and therefore, there is a conflict between action and idea. Is it possible to act immediately without idea—which is, after all, what we call love? Is it possible to see the truth of something immediately, instantly, and act instantly on that which is seen—not consider the consequences, the effect, the causes, but act instantaneously on that which has been seen as true? Do think about this.

New Delhi, 4th Public Talk, November 3, 1963
Collected Works, Vol. XIV, pp. 20-1

Action based on idea is very superficial, is not true action at all, is only ideation, which is merely the thought process going on.

What is our action at present? What do we mean by action? Our action—what we want to do or to be—is based on idea, is it not? That is all we know: we have ideas, ideals, promises, various formulas as to what we are and what we are not. The basis of our action is reward in the future or fear of punishment. We know that, don't we? Such activity is isolating, self-enclosing. You have an idea of virtue and according to that idea you live, you act, in relationship. To you, relationship, collective or individual, is action which is towards the ideal, towards virtue, towards achievement and so on.

When my action is based on an ideal which is an idea—such as "I must be brave," "I must follow the example," "I must be charitable," "I must be socially conscious," and so on—that idea shapes my action, guides my action. We all say, "There is an example of virtue which I must follow," which means, "I must live according to that." So action is based on that idea. Between action and idea, there is a gulf, a division, there is a time process. That is so, is it not? In other words, I am not charitable, I am not loving, there is no forgiveness in my heart, but I feel I must be charitable. So there is a gap between what I am and what I should be; we are all the time trying to bridge that gap. That is our activity, is it not?

Now what would happen if the idea did not exist? At one stroke, you would have removed the gap, would you not? You would be what you are. You say, "I am ugly, I must become beautiful; what am I to do?"—which is action based on idea. You say, "I am not compassionate, I must become compassionate." So you introduce idea separate from action. Therefore there is never true action of what you are but always action based on the ideal of what you will be. The stupid man always says he is going to become clever. He sits working, struggling to become; he never stops, he never says, "I am stupid." So his action, which is based on idea, is not action at all.

Action means doing, moving. But when you have idea, it is merely ideation going on, thought process going on in relation to action. If there is no idea, what would happen? You are what you are. You are uncharitable, you are unforgiving, you are cruel, stupid, thoughtless. Can you remain with that? If you do, then see what happens. When I recognize I am uncharitable, stupid, what happens when I am aware it is so? Is there not charity, is there not intelligence? When I recognize uncharitableness completely, not verbally, not artificially, when I realize I am uncharitable and unloving, in that very seeing of *what is,* is there not love? Don't I immediately become charitable? If I see the necessity of being clean, it is very simple; I go and wash. But if it is an ideal that I should be clean, then what happens? Cleanliness is then postponed or is superficial.

Action based on idea is very superficial, is not true action at all, is only ideation, which is merely the thought process going on.

The First and Last Freedom, pp. 243-4

So when you are aware of this division between idea and action, what it involves—which is, to suppress, to approximate, constantly to try and adjust action with a pattern—you see that there is never a moment when action is for itself. For me, that is one of the fundamental reasons for this disintegration, the degeneration of the mind that is in conflict, that is constantly in friction with itself.

Rajghat, Banaras, 3rd Public Talk, December 8, 1963
Collected Works, Vol. XIV, p. 69

Time arises only when there is approximation between action and idea.

For us, idea becomes extremely important, not action, and action is merely an approximation to the idea. Is it possible to act without idea and therefore no approximation at all at any time? This means really that one has to go into the question [of] why idea has taken the place of action. People talk about action: what is the right thing to do? The right thing to do is not an idea divorced from action, because then action becomes an approximation to the idea, and still the idea is important but not action. So how are you to act so completely, so totally, that there is no approximation, that you are living all the time completely? Such a person has no need of an idea, of concepts, of formulas, of methods. Then, there is no time but only action; time arises only when there is approximation between action and idea.

This may sound extravagant and absurd. But if you have gone into the question of thought, into the question of idea, and as you cannot live without action, you ask, "Is it possible to live without idea, without word, but only with action?" It is only when the mechanism of thought is understood that there is action which is not an approximation. Surely, if you think about this yourself, you will see what an extraordinary thing it is.

Rajghat, Banaras, 6th Public Talk, January 12, 1962
Collected Works, Vol. XIII, pp. 44-5

If you can listen totally to what is being said, then in that very listening you will find there is a liberation...

Please, since you have taken the trouble to come here, may I suggest that in listening to what I am saying, you listen to the end, and not just take little bits here and there which happen to suit you; listen to the totality of it, and you will see that the whole thing hangs together. If you take a little part of it, you will have only the ashes which will create more misery, more sorrow, more confusion.

Also, listening itself is quite an art. Most of us never really listen, therefore we hear only partially. We hear the words that are spoken, but our minds are elsewhere; or our minds respond only to the meaning of the words, and this immediate response prevents us from hearing that which lies beyond the words. So listening is an art; but if you can listen totally to what is being said, then in that very listening you will find there is a liberation, because such listening is unpremeditated, uncalculated; it is an action of truth because your whole mind is there, your total attention is being given. If you listen without interpreting, without remembering a quotation from some old book, or comparing all this with what you have read, then you will find that your own mind has undergone a really radical change.

Madras, 4th Public Talk, December 23, 1956
Collected Works, Vol. X, p. 185

So I would suggest this morning, as I have suggested almost every morning, that the act of listening in itself should be a total action. What is required is not fragmentary action, not action shaped to a formula and carried out by will, but action which is total; because it is total action that puts an end to all deterioration.

Saanen, 9th Public Talk, July 29, 1965
Collected Works, Vol. XV, p. 235

If we can understand action as a total thing...then that understanding will bring about right action in the particular.

If I may, I would like to think aloud about the "what to do," not only in the present but also in the future, and to consider with you the whole significance of action. But before going into that, I think we must be very clear that I am not trying to persuade you to take any particular form of action, to do this or to do that; for all persuasion, which is propaganda, whether it be considered good or bad, is essentially destructive. So let us keep very clearly in mind that you and I are thinking out the problem together, and that we are not concerned with any particular form of action, either with what to do tomorrow, or with what to do today, but if we can understand the total implication of action, then perhaps we shall be able to work out the details.

Without understanding comprehensively the full significance of action, merely to be concerned with a particular form of action seems to me very destructive. Surely, if we are concerned only with the part and not with the whole, then all action is destructive action. But if we can understand action as a total thing, if we can feel our way into it and capture its significance, then that understanding of total action will bring about right action in the particular. It is like looking at a tree; the tree is not just the leaf, the branch, the flower, the fruit, the trunk, or the root—it is a total thing. To feel the beauty of a tree is to be aware of its wholeness—the extraordinary shape of it, the depth of its shadow, the flutter of its leaves in the wind. Unless we have the feeling of the whole tree, merely looking at a single leaf will mean very little. But if we have the feeling of the whole tree, then every leaf, every twig has meaning, and we are sensitive to it. After all, to be sensitive to the beauty of something is to perceive the totality of it. The mind that is thinking in terms of a part can never perceive the whole. In the whole the part is contained, but the part will never make up the whole, the total.

New Delhi, 3rd Public Talk, February 21, 1960
Collected Works, Vol. XI, p. 341

It is only complete action that brings about intelligence.

It seems to be one of the most difficult things in life to live completely totally—not fragmentarily but as a total human being—whether you are in your office or in your home, or whether you are walking in a wood. It is only complete action that brings about intelligence: total action is intelligence. But we live in fragments: as a family man opposed to the rest of the world, as a religious man—if one is at all religious—having peculiar theories, ideas, separate beliefs and dogmas. And one is always struggling to achieve a status, a position, a prestige, whether that status is worldly or saintly. One is always striving, striving. There is never a moment when the mind is completely empty and therefore silent. And out of silence action takes place. We are no longer original. We are the result, as we have said over and over again, of our environments, of circumstances, of the culture, the tradition in which we live, and we accept that. And to change always demands a great deal of energy.

New Delhi, 4th Public Talk, December 25, 1966
Collected Works, Vol. XVII, p. 119

When one gives one's heart, it is a total action. And when you give your mind, it is a fragmentary action. And most of us give our minds to so many things. That is why we live a fragmentary life—thinking one thing and doing another; and we are torn, contradictory. To understand something, one must give not only one's mind but one's heart to it.

Madras, 1st Public Talk, December 16, 1964
Collected Works, Vol. XV, p. 6

So we are dealing not only with action, but also with compassion, because action has within it compassion.

Most of us do not think completely, but fragmentarily; what we think at one level is contradicted by our thought at another level. We feel something at a certain level and deny it at another, so our daily action is equally contradictory, fragmentary, and such action breeds conflict, misery, confusion.

Please, these are all obvious psychological facts, and to understand them you don't have to read a single book on psychology or philosophy, because there is the book inside you, the book which has been put together through centuries by man.

So we are dealing not only with action, but also with compassion, because action has within it compassion. Compassion is not something separate from action, it is not an idea to which action is approximating itself. Please do look at this, consider it carefully; because, for most of us, idea is important, and from idea there is action. But idea separated from action creates conflict. Action includes compassion; it is not just at the technological level, or at the level of relationship between husband and wife, or between the individual and the community, but it is a total movement of one's whole being. I am talking about total action, not action in fragmentation. When there is observation and therefore no observer—the observer being the idea, the word—and you begin to understand this whole complex thing called the self, the 'me', then you will know this total action, not the separative, fragmentary action in which there is conflict.

Saanen, 4th Public Talk, July 14, 1963
Collected Works, Vol. XIII, pp. 298-9

25

Let us therefore find out together what we mean by action without idea.

Questioner: For truth to come, you advocate action without idea. Is it possible to act at all times without idea, that is, without a purpose in view?

KRISHNAMURTI: I am not advocating anything. I am not a propagandist, political or religious. I am not inviting you to any new experience. All that we are doing is trying to find out what action is. You are not following me to find out. If you do, then you will never find out. You are only following me verbally. But if you want to find out, if you as an individual want to find out what idea and action are, you have to inquire into it, and not accept my definition or my experience, which may be utterly false. As you have to find out, you have to put aside the whole idea of following, pursuing, advocating, propagandist, leader or example.

Let us therefore find out together what we mean by action without idea. Please give your thought to it. Don't say, "I do not understand what you are talking about." Let us find out together. It may be difficult, but let us go into it.

Madras, 7th Public Talk, January 26, 1952
Collected Works, Vol. VI, p. 291

IV.
Impediments to Total Action

There cannot be a world transformation, a revolution, as long as action is based on ideas; because action then is merely reaction; therefore ideas become much more important than action, and that is precisely what is taking place in the world, isn't it? To act, we must discover the impediments that prevent action. But most of us don't want to act—that is our difficulty. We prefer to discuss, we prefer to substitute one ideology for another, and so we escape from action through ideology.

Colombo, Sri Lanka, 2nd Public Talk, January 1, 1950
Collected Works, Vol. VI, p. 54

A. Idea

To most of us action is not important, relationship is not important; ideas are much more important than all these other factors.

We give such extraordinary significance to thought, to ideas, to concepts, to formulas. There are physical formulas which are necessary, but are psychological formulas at all necessary?

I am not saying that we should be stupid, uninformed, dull; but why do we give such extraordinary importance to the mind, to thinking, to the intellect? If one doesn't give importance to the intellect, one gives importance either to sensate values or to the emotions. But as most people are ashamed of emotions and sensate values, they worship the intellect. Why? Please, when I ask a question, let's all of us find the answer together. Books, theories, and the whole intellectual field are considered so important in our life. Why? If you are clever, you may get a better job. If you are highly trained technologically, that may have certain advantages, but why do we give importance to ideas? Isn't it because we cannot live without action? All relationship is a movement, and that movement is action. Ideas become important when separated from action. To most of us action is not important, relationship is not important; ideas are much more important than all these other factors.

Our relationships, which comprise our life, are based on organized memory as idea. Idea dominates action; and hence relationship is a concept, not actual action. We think relationship should be this or that, but we don't actually know what relationship is. Not knowing what relationship is—actually, factually—ideas become all-important to us. The intellect becomes all-important, with its beliefs, ideas, and theories as to what should be and what should not be. Action is of a time-binding nature; that is, action involves time, because idea is of time.

Action is never immediate, never spontaneous; it is never related to *what is,* but to what should be, to an idea, and hence there is a conflict between idea and action.

London, 6th Public Dialogue, May 9, 1965
Collected Works, Vol. XV, p. 141

I think it is important to find out why human beings throughout the ages have given such an extraordinary importance to ideas.

It is very important to understand why we create or formulate an idea. Why does the mind formulate an idea at all? I mean by "formulating" a structure of philosophical or rational or humanistic or materialistic ideas. Idea is organized thought; and in that organized thought, belief, idea, man lives. That is what we all do, whether we are religious or non-religious. I think it is important to find out why human beings throughout the ages have given such an extraordinary importance to ideas. Why do we formulate ideas at all? ...We form ideas, if one observes oneself, when there is inattention. When you are completely active, which demands total attention—which is action—in that there is no idea; you are acting.

Bombay, 7th Public Talk, March 3, 1965
Collected Works, Vol. XV, p. 89

Can ideas ever produce action, or do ideas merely mold thought and therefore limit action?

If we can understand action in the fundamental sense of the word then that fundamental understanding will affect our superficial activities also; but first we must understand the fundamental nature of action. Now is action brought about by an idea? Do you have an idea first and act afterwards? Or does action come first and then, because action creates conflict, you build around it an idea? Does action create the actor or does the actor come first?

It is very important to discover which comes first. If the idea comes first, then action merely conforms to an idea, and therefore it is no longer action but imitation, compulsion according to an idea. It is very important to realize this; because, as our society is mostly constructed on the intellectual or verbal level, the idea comes first with all of us and action follows. Action is then the handmaid of an idea, and the mere construction of ideas is obviously detrimental to action. Ideas breed further ideas, and when there is merely the breeding of ideas there is antagonism, and society becomes top-heavy with the intellectual process of ideation. Our social structure is very intellectual; we are cultivating the intellect at the expense of every other factor of our being and therefore we are suffocated with ideas.

Can ideas ever produce action, or do ideas merely mold thought and therefore limit action? When action is compelled by an idea, action can never liberate man. It is extraordinarily important for us to understand this point. If an idea shapes action, then action can never bring about the solution to our miseries because, before it can be put into action, we have first to discover how the idea comes into being. The investigation of ideation, of the building up of ideas—whether of the socialists, the capitalists, the communists, or of the various religions—is of the utmost importance, especially when our society is at the edge of a precipice, inviting another catastrophe, another excision. Those who are really serious in their intention to discover the human solution to our many problems must first understand this process of ideation.

What do we mean by an idea? How does an idea come into being? And can idea and action be brought together? Suppose I have an idea and I wish to carry it out. I seek a method of carrying out that idea, and we speculate, waste our time and energies in quarrelling over how the idea should be carried out. So it is really very important to find out how ideas come into being; and after discovering the truth of that we can discuss the question of action. Without discussing ideas, merely to find out how to act has no meaning.

Now, how do you get an idea—a very simple idea, it need not be philosophical, religious or economic? Obviously it is a process of thought, is it not? Idea is the outcome of a thought process. Without a thought process, there can be no idea. So I have to understand the thought process itself before I can understand its product, the idea. What do we mean by thought ? When do you think? Obviously thought is the result of a response, neurological or psychological, is it not? It is the immediate response of the senses to a sensation, or it is psychological, the response of stored-up memory. There is the immediate response of the nerves to a sensation, and there is the psychological response of stored-up memory, the influence of race, group, guru, family, tradition, and so on—all of which you call thought. So the thought process is the response of memory, is it not? You would have no thoughts if you had no memory, and the response of memory to a certain experience brings the thought process into action.

The First and Last Freedom, pp. 52-3

99.9 percent of our actions are an approximation of a belief, an idea, a concept, an image.

I have to act with regard to the fact, with regard to *what is,* with regard to what I find. There must be action, and I have to investigate and understand what is meant by action. If I don't understand that fully, if I am concerned with changing the fact, with doing something about it, I can't face the fact. I must understand what action is; and 99.9 percent of our actions are an approximation of a belief, an idea, a concept, an image. Our action is always trying to copy, to conform to an idea. I have an idea that I should be brotherly; I have an idea as a communist; or I have the idea that I am a Catholic—according to the idea, I act. I have certain memories of pleasure or of pain, certain remembrances of some deep fear, an image of that fear; and according to those memories I act, avoiding some particular issues, and acting for profit, for a deeper happiness. All of this is ideation, and according to that ideation, I act. When there is an idea, and action, there is conflict between the two. The idea is the observer, and the act of what I am going to do is the object.

Saanen, 3rd Public Discussion, August 5, 1966
Collected Works, Vol. XVI, p. 268

When we see that action is approximating itself to an idea and therefore it is not an action, then we will put away all idea and know what action is.

Questioner: In a little village there is a poisonous snake, and there is a woman crying her heart out because the snake has bitten her baby and the baby is dead. I can kill the snake or I can leave it alone. What am I to do?

KRISHNAMURTI: What do you do? Do you wait until you come to this tent to be told what to do? Or do you do something there? You act! If you are callous, indifferent, you don't do anything; if you are moved, you actually, immediately, do something. Sir, all our activity is based on the idea that we must help, that we must be good, that this is right, and that is wrong. All action is conditioned by an idea, by our country, by our culture, by the food we eat. All that conditions our actions because they are based on an idea. When we see that action is approximating itself to an idea and therefore it is not an action, then we will put away all idea and know what action is. It is very interesting to observe how we have broken up action: righteous, immoral, right, true, noble, ignoble, national action, action according to the church. If we understand the worthlessness of such action, then we act. We do not ask how to act, what to do; we act and that act is the most beautiful act at that moment.

Saanen, 8th Public Talk, July 26, 1966
Collected Works, Vol. XVI, p. 241

B. Beliefs, ideologies, commitments

You are violent...Why can't you look at that violence? Why need you have an ideal of non-violence?

Look, sirs, you have been brought up, most unfortunately, on ideals. Ideals are just words. They have no meaning whatsoever, they have no substance. They are just the barren children of a vain, thoughtless mind! You have been brought up on the ideal of non-violence. You go around preaching all over the world non-violence. Non-violence is the ideal. But the fact is that you are violent in your gesture, in the way you talk to your superior or your inferior. Please listen to yourself. I am just pointing it out. You are violent—violent in your gesture, in your thought, in your feeling, in your action. Why can't you look at that violence? Why need you have an ideal of non-violence? The fact is you are violent, and the ideal is non-factual; so you create a contradiction in yourself and therefore prevent yourself from looking at the fact of violence. When you look at a fact you can deal with it: you will say you are violent and accept it; you accept it and say, "I am violent and I will not be a hypocrite," or you will say you are violent and enjoy it, or you will look at it without the ideal. You can only look at an object or a fact or *what is*, when there is no ideal, no opinion, no judgment—it is so. Then the fact brings about an intensity of action in the immediate. It is only when you have ideas about a fact that you postpone action. When you realize factually that you are violent, then you can look at it, you can go into it; then you can learn all about it, the nature of violence, whether it is possible to be free or not—not as an idea, but actually. So a religious mind has no ideals, no example, no authority, because the fact is the only thing that matters, and that fact demands urgency of action.

Madras, 4th Public Talk, December 27, 1964
Collected Works, Vol. XV, p. 25

It is very difficult not to be a communist, a socialist, this or that, and to inquire into what is total action. Most of us are committed to something or other, and a man who is committed to something is incapable of learning. Life never stands still, it does not commit itself to anything, it is in eternal movement. And you want to translate this living thing in terms of a particular belief or ideology, which is utterly childish.

New Delhi, 2nd Public Talk, February 11, 1959
Collected Works, Vol. XI, p. 164

The ideal becomes a distraction; the ideal is a fiction, a myth; it is not a reality.

Now when you observe why the idea becomes important, when you are aware why the pattern has assumed such an extraordinary significance, you can see why it does. Because, first of all, it tends to postpone action: I am violent and I have this marvelous idea of non-violence, which is an ideal, and I can pursue that ideal and not act because I am still trying to be non-violent. Therefore, it is an escape from the fact of violence. If I have no ideal of non-violence, I can deal with the fact.

So the ideal becomes a distraction; the ideal is a fiction, a myth; it is not a reality. The reality is *what is*, which is violence. And we think that by having an ideal like non-violence, we can push violence out of ourselves—which never takes place, which can never take place. Because when we deal with facts alone, there is an operation, not when we deal with ideas. So that is one of the reasons: an idea or a pattern offers a means of postponing, of escaping from the fact; and the idea becomes important to give continuity to a particular act. I did this yesterday, I will do this today and tomorrow—it gives a continuity or becomes a habit which prevents action. This is merely carrying out a certain formula and therefore it becomes mechanical. Life is not mechanical; it has to be lived, it is action changing every minute.

So ideas offer a means of postponing action. Therefore the more ideas, the more ideals you have, the more inactive you are. Please do see this: when you act from an idea you are not active, because you are living your life in a world of fiction without any reality. So escape, postponement, offering a continuity, which gives you a habit, and functioning from a habit—that is memory and therefore mechanical. So you can see, ideas do not bring passion. I think it is very important to understand this: to act, you must have passion; to do, you must have strong feelings; otherwise, it becomes mechanical. You cannot have strong, intense, immediate feeling and passion if you have ideas.

Rajghat, Banaras, 3rd Public Talk, December 8, 1963
Collected Works, Vol. XIV, pp. 69-70

The idealist is the man with an idea, and it is he who is not revolutionary. Ideas divide, and separation is disintegration, it is not revolution at all. The man with an ideology is concerned with ideas, words, and not with direct action; he avoids direct action. An ideology is a hindrance to direct action.

Commentaries on Living, Series II, p. 16

So the desire, the urge to do something, makes us commit ourselves to a particular course of action. We don't look to see whether that course of action includes the totality of man.

Why is it that we have this urge to commit ourselves to something? One cause of this urge, surely, is that we see confusion, misery, degradation, and we want to do something about it; and there are people who are already doing something about it. The communists, the socialists, the various political parties and religious groups—they all claim to be doing something to save the poor, to bring food, clothing, and shelter to the needy. They talk about the welfare of the people, and they are very convincing. Many of them sacrifice, practice austerities, work from morning till night at something or other; and seeing them we say, "What extraordinary people they are." Because we want to help, we join them—and so we have committed ourselves. Just follow the sequence of it. After having committed ourselves to a party or a movement, we look at everything through that particular window, in terms of that particular course of action, and we don't want to be disturbed. Previously we were disturbed; but now, having committed ourselves, we are in a state of comparative tranquillity, and we don't want to be disturbed again. But there are other parties and movements, all claiming the same thing, each with a clever leader who manifests an extraordinary, recognizable rectitude.

So the desire, the urge to do something, makes us commit ourselves to a particular course of action. We don't look to see whether that course of action includes the totality of man. Do you understand? I will explain what I mean. Any particular course of action is exclusive, and is therefore concerned only with a part of man. It is not concerned with the whole man—with his mind, his human quality, his goodness, and all that. It is a partial, not a total concern.

And we commit ourselves, not only to a particular course of action, but also to a particular belief or way of life. The man who becomes a sannyasi, a monk, a saint, has taken a vow to be celibate, to live in poverty, to offer prayers, to be this and not to be that; he has committed himself to that pattern. Why? Because it is a marvelous escape, a way of resolving all his problems by avoiding the constant lapping of life on the banks of his mind. He does not understand this movement of life, he does not know what it is all about, but at least his self-discipline and his belief give him a sense of safety, security, and there is always Jesus, or Buddha, or God at the end of it; so the man who is committed to such a course is perfectly happy. He says, "What is there to doubt? It is all quite clear. Come and join us, and you too will know all about it." All this I have not said cynically or harshly. I am just pointing out, not criticizing, and you are just looking.

Rajghat, Banaras, 4th Public Talk, February 7, 1960
Collected Works, Vol. XI, p. 324

Aloneness implies an awareness of all the different implications of the various forms of commitments of man out of his confusion.

Can we this evening find out for ourselves whether it is possible for a mind which realizes that it is confused, realizes it is committed to a particular course of action, social or religious, to cease to be committed; not because someone tells it to do so, but through understanding

35

that any commitment to any particular pattern of thought or action engenders more confusion? If a mind demands clarity, demands that it be free from all confusion because it understands the necessity of freedom, that very understanding frees the mind from commitment, and that's one of the most difficult things to do. We are committed because we think that commitment will lead us to a certain clarity, to a certain facility of action. And if we are not committed, we feel lost, because all around us people are committed. We go to this group or to that group, to this teacher or to that teacher; we follow a certain leader. Everyone is caught in this, and not to be committed demands the awareness of what is implied in commitment. If we are aware of a danger and see it very clearly, then we don't touch it; we don't go near it. But to see it clearly is very difficult because the mind says, "I must do, act; I can't wait. What am I to do?" Surely, a mind that is confused, uncertain, disturbed, must first realize that it is disturbed, and also understand that any movement of this disturbance only creates further disturbance. Not to be committed implies to stand completely alone; and that demands great understanding of fear. We can see what's happening in the world. No one wants to be alone. I do not mean alone with a radio, with a book, sitting under a tree by yourself, or in a monastery with a different name or a different label. Aloneness implies an awareness of all the different implications of the various forms of commitments of man out of his confusion. When a mature human being demands freedom from confusion, then there is that awareness of the facts of confusion. Out of that there is an aloneness; then one is alone; then one is really not afraid.

What are we to do? We see very clearly that any action born of confusion only leads to more confusion. That's very simple and very clear. Then what is right action? We live by action. We cannot but act. The whole process of living is action. We must again go into this question of what action is. We know very clearly the action born of confusion, through which act we hope to achieve certainty, clarity. If we see that, then, not being committed to any course of thought, philosophy or ideals, what is action? This is a legitimate question after we have said all these things.

New York, 3rd Public Talk, September 30, 1966
Collected Works, Vol. XVII, pp. 17-8

C. Reaction and the process of thought

The idea, the concept, the pattern is born of our thinking, which in turn is based upon our conditioning. All our thinking, however noble, refined or subtle, is the outcome of our experience, of our knowledge. There is no thinking without the past. Our thought is merely the reaction of memory. And what I am talking about is action without reaction, which means living without thought as the reaction of memory.

Saanen, 4th Public Talk, June 29, 1962
Collected Works, Vol. XIII, p. 233

Reaction leads to incomplete action and therefore to the continuity of more conflict, more misery.

So a mind is concerned with itself, as most people are. You have to be concerned with yourselves at one level, physiologically—earning a [living]. But the self-concern at a deeper level, at the deep psychological level, breeds inaction, which is laziness. Psychologically, inwardly, if you have observed yourself and the world about you, you see that your action is merely a reaction, all your activities are a reaction, are a response to likes or dislikes.

Please follow this a little bit, because I want to show that there is an activity which is not the result of reaction or the result of an idea. I want to show that there is an action which is the outcome of total negation of reaction, and therefore such action is creative action. To understand that, to go into that question—which is really not complex, but is an extraordinary state of mind—you have to understand your reactions from which your daily action springs. We react, we revolt, we accumulate, we defend, we resist, we acquire, we submit—all these are reactions.

I say something to you; you don't like it, and you do something in response to that which you don't like to accept. At that level we are acting all the time. You have been brought up, conditioned to a particular pattern of life; that is your daily life, pattern of life, inwardly and outwardly. And when that is questioned, you revolt, you react according to your conditioning, according to your habits; from that reaction there is another action. So we move from reaction to reaction all the time, and therefore we never are free. That is one of the origins of sorrow. Please understand this.

There must be reaction. When you see something ugly, it must react; when you see something beautiful, it must react; when you see a poisonous snake, it must react; otherwise you are dead, you are insensitive, you are not alive, you are dull. But that reaction is different from the reaction which society and yourself, through experiences, have built up, which has become your conditioning. When you see a tree, when you see a sunset, if you do not react, you are paralyzed. But when you react according to self-pity, according to your conclusions, according to your habits, according to your failures, successes, hopes, despairs, such reaction leads to incomplete action and therefore to the continuity of more conflict, more misery.

I hope you see the difference between the two kinds of reaction. The reaction which sees and does not translate what it sees in terms of its own conditioning—that is one kind of reaction; that is the real action. And the other kind of reaction is that which sees and says, "That is beautiful, I must have it," that reaction is the response of its own conditioning, memory, of its own self-pity, of its own desires, and all the rest of it. So please see the difference between these two.

Bombay, 5th Public Talk, March 4, 1962
Collected Works, Vol. XIII, pp. 141-2

In that state of mind which is reacting, can you observe anything?

We act: our action, as it is now, is a reaction, isn't it? A insults B, B reacts, and that reaction is his action. If A flatters B, then also B reacts, and his action is a reaction. B is pleased with it; he remembers that he is a good man, he is a friend, and all the rest of it; and from that there is a subsequent action, which is: A influences B, and B reacts to that influence, and from that reaction is further action. So, that is the process we know, a positive influence, a response which may be the positive continued or the opposite negative action—reaction and action. In that way we function. And when we say, "I must be free from something," it is still within the field of it; when I say, "I must be free from anger, from vanity," the desire to be free is a reaction. Because anger, vanity, might have brought you misery, discomfort, you say, "I must not be that." So the "must not" is a reaction to "what was" or "what is," and from that negative there is a series of actions as discipline, control—"I must not," "I must." From an influence, from a conditioning, there is a reaction, and that reaction creates further action. Therefore, there is a positive and a negative response, a positive push and a negative push; and from the negative push there is a response, an answer, an action. Now in that state of mind which is reacting, can you observe anything?

Bombay, 6th Public Talk, March 3, 1961
Collected Works, Vol. XII, pp. 82-3

Do you understand what I mean by a reaction? You insult me, you say something which I don't like, and I react; or I like what you say, and again I react. But is it not possible to listen to what another says without reacting? Surely, if I listen to find out the truth or the falseness of what you are saying, then from that listening, from that perception, there is an action which is not reaction.

Saanen, 4th Public Talk, July 29, 1962
Collected Works, Vol. XIII, p. 233

If we know how to listen, that very listening is an action in which the miracle of understanding takes place.

If I may turn aside for a moment, I think it is important to understand what it means to listen, for then, perhaps, what is being said will have a meaning beyond the words. It seems to me that very few of us ever do listen. We do not know how to listen. I wonder if you have ever really listened to your child, to your wife or husband, or to a bird? I wonder if you have ever listened to the mind as it watches a sunset, or if you have read a poem with an attitude of listening? If we know how to listen, that very listening is an action in which the miracle of understanding takes place. If we know how to listen to what is being said, we shall discover whether it is true or false. And what is true, one does not have to accept: it is so. It is only when there is contention between the false and the false that there is acceptance and rejection, agreement and disagreement.

New Delhi, 5th Public Talk, February 28, 1960
Collected Works, Vol. XI, pp. 352-3

Thought is essentially born of choice...any action born of such thought...will produce sorrow, misery, not only for me but for others as well.

So what we are trying to do is to feel out the totality of action. There is no action without the background of thought, is there? And thought is always choice. Don't just accept this. Please examine it, feel your way into it. Thought is the process of choosing. Without thought you cannot choose. The moment you choose, there is a decision, and that decision creates its own opposite—good and bad, violence and non-violence. The man who pursues non-violence through decision creates a contradiction in himself. Thought is essentially born of choice; I choose to think in a certain way. I examine communism, socialism, Buddhism; I reason logically and decide to think this or that. Such thought is based on memory, on my conditioning, on my pleasure, on my likes and dislikes, and any action born of such thought will inevitably create contradiction in myself and therefore in the world; it will produce sorrow, misery, not only for me but for others as well.

New Delhi, 2nd Public Talk, February 11, 1959
Collected Works, Vol. XI, p. 164

An action which is without choice does not breed conflict.

The computer is going to take charge of all the drudgery of man, in the office and also politically; it is going to do all the work for human beings, in the factories. And so man will have a great deal of leisure. That is a fact. You may not see it in the immediate, but it is there, coming. There is a tremendous wave, and you are going to have a choice to make: what you will do with your time.

We said "choice"—to choose between various forms of amusement, entertainment; in which is included all the religious phenomena—temples, mass, reading scriptures. All these are forms of entertainment! Please don't laugh; what we are talking about is much too serious. You have no time to laugh when the house is burning. Only we refuse to think of what is actually taking place. And you are going to have the choice—this or that? And when choice is involved, there is always conflict. That is, when you have two ways of action, that choice merely produces more conflict. But if you saw very clearly within yourself—as a human being belonging to the whole world, not just to one petty, little country in some little geographical division, or class division, or Brahmin, or non-Brahmin, and all the rest of it—if you saw this issue clearly, then there would be no choice. Therefore an action which is without choice does not breed conflict.

Madras, 2nd Public Talk, December 26, 1965
Collected Works, Vol. XVI, p. 9

What we are trying to find out is whether it is possible for action to be without idea?

What do we mean by idea? Surely idea is the process of thought, is it not? Idea is a process of mentation, of thinking; and thinking is always a reaction either of the conscious or of the unconscious. Thinking is a process of verbalization which is the result of memory—thinking is a process of time. So when action is based on the process of thinking, such action must inevitably be conditioned, isolated. Idea must oppose idea, idea must be dominated by idea. There is a gap then between action and idea. What we are trying to find out is whether it is possible for action to be without idea. We see how idea separates people. As I have already explained, knowledge and belief are essentially separating qualities. Beliefs never bind people; they always separate people; when action is based on belief or an idea or an ideal, such action must inevitably be isolated, fragmented. Is it possible to act without the process of thought, thought being a process of time, a process of calculation, a process of self-protection, a process of belief, denial, condemnation, justification? Surely, it must have occurred to you as it has to me, whether action is at all possible without idea. I see, as well as you see, that when I have an idea and I base my action on that idea, it must create opposition; idea must meet idea and must inevitably create suppression, opposition. I do not know if I am making myself clear. To me this is really a very important point. If you can understand that, not by the mind or sentimentally but intimately, I feel we shall have transcended all our difficulties. Our difficulties are of ideas, not of action. It is not what we should do, which is merely an idea; what is important is acting. Is action possible without the process of calculation, which is the result of self-protection, of memory, of relationship—personal, individual, collective, and so on? I say it is possible. You can experiment with it when you are here.

Madras, 3rd Public Talk, January 12, 1952
Collected Works, Vol. VI, p. 260

When you have gone through the whole process of action born of reaction, and denied it with enchantment, with joy...

So action which is born of reaction breeds sorrow. Most of our thoughts are the result of the past, of time. A mind that is not built on the past, that has totally understood this whole process of reaction, can act every minute totally, completely, wholly.

Please do listen. What I am going to say will probably be rather difficult. So, listen as though you are far away. I am going to talk about something which you will come to, if you have gone through all this sweetly, with pleasure. When you have gone through the whole process of action born of reaction, and denied it with enchantment, with joy—not with pain—then you will see that you will come naturally, easily, to a state of mind that is the very essence of beauty.

Bombay, 5th Public Talk, March 4, 1962
Collected Works, Vol. XIII, p. 143

D. Effort, will

Is it possible to understand anything without effort? Is it possible to see what is real, what is true, without introducing the action of will?

Perhaps this evening we could go into the problem of effort. It seems to me that it is very important to understand the approach we make to any conflict, to any problem with which we are faced. We are concerned, are we not, most of us, with the action of will. And to us, effort is most essential in every form; to us, to live without effort seems incredible, leading to stagnation and to deterioration. And if we can go into that problem of effort, I think perhaps it will be profitable; because we may then be able to understand what is truth, without exercising will, without making an effort, by being capable of perceiving directly *what is*. But to do that, we must understand this question of effort, and I hope we can go into it without any opposition, any resistance.

For most of us, our whole life is based on effort, some kind of volition. And we cannot conceive of an action without volition, without effort; our life is based on it. Our social, economic, and so-called spiritual life is a series of efforts, always culminating in a certain result. And we think effort is essential, necessary. So, we are now going to find out if it is possible to live differently, without this constant battle.

Why do we make effort? Is it not, put simply, in order to achieve a result, to become something, to reach a goal? And if we do not make an effort, we think we shall stagnate. We have an idea about the goal towards which we are constantly striving, and this striving has become part of our life. If we want to alter ourselves, if we want to bring about a radical change in ourselves, we make a tremendous effort to eliminate the old habits, to resist the habitual environmental influences, and so on. So we are used to this series of efforts in order to find or achieve something—in order to live at all.

And is not all such effort the activity of the self? Is not effort self-centered activity? And if we make an effort from the center of the self, it must inevitably produce more conflict, more confusion, more misery. Yet we keep on making effort after effort. And very few of us realize that the self-centered activity of effort does not clear up any of our problems. On the contrary, it increases our confusion and our misery and our sorrow. We know this. And yet we continue hoping somehow to break through this self-centered activity of effort, the action of the will.

That is our problem: is it possible to understand anything without effort? Is it possible to see what is real, what is true, without introducing the action of will?—which is essentially based on the self, the 'me'. And if we do not make an effort, is there not a danger of deterioration, of going to sleep, of stagnation? Perhaps this evening, as I am talking, we can experiment with this individually, and see how far we can go through this question. For I feel the thing that brings happiness, quietness, tranquillity of the mind, does not come through any effort. A truth is not perceived through any volition, through any action of will. And if we can go into it very carefully and diligently, perhaps we shall find the answer.

London, 5th Public Talk, April 23, 1952
Collected Works, Vol. VI, pp. 354-5

Having created the idea, we proceed to put that idea into action. Then we try to bridge the gap between idea and action—in which effort is involved.

How do we react when a truth is presented? Take, for example, what we were discussing the other day—the problem of fear. We realize that our activity and our being and our whole existence would be fundamentally altered if there were no fear of any kind in us. We may see that, we may see the truth of it; and thereby there is a freedom from fear. But for most of us, when a fact, a truth, is put before us, what is our immediate response? Please experiment with what I am saying; please do not merely listen. Watch your own reactions and find out what happens when a truth, a fact, is put before you—such as, "Any dependency in relationship destroys relationship." Now, when a statement of that kind is made, what is your response? Do you see, are you aware of the truth of it, and thereby dependency ceases? Or have you an idea about the fact? Here is a statement of truth. Do we experience the truth of it, or do we create an idea about it?

If we can understand the process of this creation of idea, then we shall perhaps understand the whole process of effort. Because when once we have created the idea, then effort comes into being. Then the problem arises, what to do, how to act? That is, we see that psychological dependency on another is a form of self-fulfillment; it is not love; in it there is conflict, in it there is fear, in it there is dependency, which corrodes; in it there is the desire to fulfill oneself through another, jealousy, and so on. We see that psychological dependency on another embraces all these facts. Then we proceed to create the idea, do we not? We do not directly experience the fact, the truth of it; but we look at it, and then create an idea of how to be free from dependency. We see the implications of psychological dependence, and then we create the idea of how to be free from it. We do not directly experience the truth, which is the liberating factor. But out of the experience of looking at that fact, we create an idea. We are incapable of looking at it directly, without ideation. Then, having created the idea, we proceed to put that idea into action. Then we try to bridge the gap between idea and action—in which effort is involved.

London, 5th Public Talk, April 23, 1952
Collected Works, Vol. VI, pp. 355-6

To live with effort is evil; to me it is an abomination.

As I was saying, if we do not understand the nature of effort, all action is limiting. Effort creates its own frontiers, its own objectives, its own limitations. Effort has the time-binding quality. You say, "I must meditate, I must make an effort to control my mind." That very effort to control puts a limit on your mind. Do watch this, do think it out with me. To live with effort is evil; to me it is an abomination, if I may use a strong word. And if you observe, you will realize that from childhood on we are conditioned to make an effort. In our so-called education, in all the work we do, we struggle to improve ourselves, to become something. Everything we undertake is based on effort; and the more effort we make, the duller the mind becomes.

* * * * *

Where there is effort, there is an objective; where there is effort, there is a limitation on attention and on action. To do good in the wrong direction is to do evil. Do you understand? For centuries we have done "good" in the wrong direction by assuming that we must be this, we must not be that, and so on, which only creates further conflict.

Madras, 4th Public Talk, December 2, 1959
Collected Works, Vol. XI, pp. 229-30, 233

Self-contradiction is the cause of your ceaseless effort.

Self-contradiction does produce action, does it not? And the more determined you are in your self-contradiction, the more energy you pour into action. Do watch this process in yourself. The tension of self-contradiction produces its own action. If you are a clerk and you want to be the manager, or you want to become a famous artist or writer, or a great saint, in that state of self-contradiction you act most vigorously, and your action is praised by society, which is equally in a state of self-contradiction. You are this, which you dislike, and you want to become that, which you like. So, self-contradiction is the cause of your ceaseless effort. Don't say, "How am I to get out of self-contradiction?" That is a most silly question to ask. Just see how completely you are caught up in self-contradiction. That is enough; because the moment you are fully aware of the contradiction in yourself, with all its implications, that very awareness creates the energy to be free of contradiction. Awareness of the fact, like awareness of a dangerous thing, creates its own energy, which in turn produces action not based on contradiction.

Bombay, 2nd Public Talk, December 27, 1959
Collected Works, Vol. XI, pp. 262-3

Total revolution must be wholly unconscious, not voluntary, not brought about by any action of the will.

We use virtue, "love," the action of the will, as a means of conquering ourselves, our idiosyncracies, and we think we are changing. But, essentially, when we go down to deeper layers, there it is still the same. When we are considering revolution, change, surely we are not concerned only with superficial changes, which are necessary, but with the deeper issue—which is the revolution, total revolution, the integrated revolution of our whole being. Can that change be brought about by effort, or must there be a cessation of all effort?

What does effort mean? With most of us, effort implies the action of the will, does it not? I hope you are following all this, because if you do not listen wisely, you will miss totally what I am going to say. If you listen wisely, you will directly experience what I am talking about. Total revolution must be wholly unconscious, not voluntary, not brought about by any action of the will. Will is still the desire, still the 'me', the self, at whatever level you may place that will. The will of action is still the desire and, therefore, it is still the 'me', and when I suppress myself in order to be good, in order to achieve, in order to become more noble, it is still desire, it is still the action of the will trying to transform itself, to put on a different clothing, it is still the will of the 'me' trying to achieve a result.

Madras, 6th Public Talk, December 20, 1953
Collected Works, Vol. VIII, p. 35

Will is the outcome of desire.

As long as the mind is seeking, there must be endeavor, effort, which is invariably based on the action of will, and however refined, will is the outcome of desire. Will may be the outcome of many integrated desires, or of a single desire, and that will expresses itself through action, does it not? When you say you are seeking truth, behind all the meditation, the devotion, the discipline entailed in that search, there is surely this action of will, which is desire...

Rajghat, Banaras, 2nd Public Talk, December 18, 1955
Collected Works, Vol. IX, p. 179

In the action of will, one dominant desire is imposing itself upon other desires.

...when we try to break down our conditioning through the action of will, what happens? One desire becomes dominant and resists the various other desires—which means that there is always the whole problem of suppression, resistance, and so-called sublimation. Does any of this free the mind from conditioning?

I wonder if we fully understand the implication of using the will to get rid of something, or to become something. What is will? Surely will is, in itself, a way of conditioning the mind, is it not? In the action of will, one dominant desire is imposing itself upon other desires, one wish is over-riding other motives and urges. This process obviously creates inward opposition, and hence there is ever conflict. So, will cannot help us to free the mind.

Stockholm, Sweden, 6th Public Talk, May 25, 1956
Collected Works, Vol. X, p. 26

You see how in everything you do there is the effort to change—which is the will of action—and as you listen very quietly, you see that the will of action comes to an end.

...I say change is possible without the action of will. That is the only change, none other is change, none other is revolution. But to understand that, it requires a great deal of insight, a great deal of meditation—not the meditation of shutting eyes, gazing at a picture or image, or an imaginary phrase; but the meditation that reveals this whole process of effort.

That is, if you are really listening now to what I am saying, you will be meditating; you are meditating, because through that listening, that watchful observation of what I am saying and [through] watching your own mind in operation, you see how in everything you do there is the effort to change—which is the will of action—and as you listen very quietly, you see that the will of action comes to an end. Therefore, with that very ending of the will to act is the beginning of radical transformation.

* * * * *

So the mind becomes innocent, free; and it is only in such a free, innocent mind that reality can come into being. No search under the will of action can make the mind tranquil; the mind is tranquil only when it has understood the whole process of the will, the action of the will to be. The will to change comes to an end not through any form of compulsion but only when the mind really understands. When it is understood, there is an astonishing change, a revolution which is transcendental, which is not of the mind. It is only that revolution that can build a new house; and without that revolution, they labor in vain that build, they are mischief makers, they produce sorrow, they multiply problems. Therefore, it is very important for you and me to understand this whole problem of effort.

Madras, 6th Public Talk, December 20, 1953
Collected Works, Vol. VIII, pp. 37, 38

E. Time, the postponement of action

If you realize there is no time excepting the chronological time, then you are faced with solving the problem immediately, not postponing it.

Why does the mind create this time, this time of the future, tomorrow, the next moment? Why do you say that you will do something tomorrow? Why do you say that you will give up smoking? The will—that is, "I will do something"—which is in time, in the future, is thought out by the mind. When you say, "I will do" or "I will try," when you say, "In the meantime"—all those indicate that you are dealing with an artificial time, but not with chronological time. So the mind invents time first as a postponement—please listen to this—as a means of postponing action. All our education is geared to the future, because we are so dissatisfied with the present that we do not understand the present. The present is too complex. The present demands that you give your total attention to everything that you do, to all the thoughts, to all the feelings; it demands the care of everything that you do, the care of your word, the care of your gesture, how you talk, how you look—that demands tremendous energy, that demands great attention.

* * * * *

But if one realizes that there is no psychological tomorrow, no tomorrow, then the thought will never say, "I will": "I will be kind," "I will be generous," "I will be honest," or "I will be less corrupt." When the mind sees clearly this whole question of time as gradation, as gradualness, as a means of gradual progress, then time becomes totally unreal; then you are faced only with the actual chronological time, and there is no other time. Then your whole action is different. The mind has to realize that there is no tomorrow, [only] an invented tomorrow.

You have many problems that you think you will solve by investigating, by postponing, by asking somebody what to do about it, or by the slow process of analysis—which are all the process of time. If you realize there is no time excepting the chronological time, then you are faced with solving the problem immediately, not postponing it. Sirs, when you have a problem of hunger or a problem of lust—those are very demanding problems—you do not say, "I will eat tomorrow," "I will satisfy my sexual appetite another day," because they are very urgent, they demand immediate action. But we human beings have invented this time as a means of postponing, as a means of not coming directly into contact with the problem, as a means of evasion.

New Delhi, 5th Public Talk, November 5, 1964
Collected Works, Vol. XIV, pp. 253-4

When something can be done immediately—and all action is in the immediate—why introduce the interval of time?

When you say, "I will change," there is a time interval, is there not? When you say, "I will do that tomorrow," there is a time interval, isn't there? I say that the time interval is a waste of energy. That is, when something can be done immediately—and all action is in the immediate—why introduce the interval of time? Why do you say, "I will do it"? Take this, for instance, sir: one is angry or jealous. Why don't you deal with that fact immediately? Why do you allow a time interval by saying, "I will do it tomorrow," "I will get rid of it tomorrow"? Why? Because you are so used to postponing, you are so used to the habit of saying, "I will do it." So gradually you have increased the time interval so that you can carry on with the thing you want to do—which may be harmful; but you like it, and therefore you carry on. Why pretend?

Rajghat, Banaras, 3rd Public Talk, November 24, 1964
Collected Works, Vol. XIV, pp. 295

Is there an ending to time? If the mind can discover it, understand it, then action has a totally different meaning.

Is there time? Because if there is no ending to time, there is no freedom, there is no end to sorrow; then life is merely [a] series of continuous reactions, responses, and so on. So is there an ending to time? If the mind can discover it, understand it, then action has a totally different meaning. Right? Sir, if you are told that your house is on fire, you will not be sitting here! If you are told that there is no tomorrow, you will be horrified! There is a tomorrow chronologically, but there will be no psychological tomorrow. And if there is no tomorrow, it is a tremendous revolution inwardly. Then love, action, beauty, space, freedom—these have a totally different meaning.

Madras, 4th Public Talk, January 2, 1966
Collected Works, Vol. XVI, p. 22

So we are concerned with time. And we say time is the interval between actions. A mind that is in action can be without time. Please follow this. A mind that is in action with an idea, with a motive, with a purpose, with a formula, is caught in time; and therefore that action, being incomplete, gives continuity to time.

Bombay, 5th Public Talk, February 23, 1964
Collected Works, Vol. XIV, p. 150

Is it possible to live in this world without giving continuity to action, so that one comes to every action afresh?

Now, to find out if there is such a thing as the eternal, one has to understand what is time. Time is a most extraordinary thing—and I am not talking about chronological time, time by the watch, which is both obvious and necessary. I am talking about time as psychological continuity. And is it possible to live without that continuity? What gives continuity, surely, is thought. If one thinks about something constantly, it has a continuity. If one looks at a picture of one's wife every day, one gives it a continuity. And is it possible to live in this world without giving continuity to action, so that one comes to every action afresh? That is, can I die to each action throughout the day, so that the mind never accumulates and is therefore never contaminated by the past, but is always new, fresh, innocent? I say that such a thing is possible, that one can live in this way—but that does not mean it is real for you. You have to find out for yourself.

Saanen, 10th Public Talk, August 2, 1964
Collected Works, Vol. XIV, pp. 222-3

V.
Total Action

Find out for yourself what is this extraordinary thing, an action which is total.

Is there an action which is not the outcome of choice, of ideation, of a decision, but is the total feeling of action? I say there is. As we are living now, the government does one thing, the business-man does another, the religious man, the scholar and the scientist—each does something else, and they are all in contradiction. These contradictions can never be overcome, because the overcoming of a contradiction only creates another tension. The essential thing is for the mind to understand the totality of action, that is, to get the feeling of action which is not born of decision, as one might get the feeling of a lovely sunset, of a flower, or a bird on the wing. This requires an inquiry into the unconscious with no positive demand for an answer. And if you are capable of not being caught up in the immediacy of life, of what to do tomorrow, then you will find that the mind begins to discover a state of action in which there is no contradiction, an action which has no opposite. You try it. Try it as you go home, when you are sitting in the bus. Find out for yourself what is this extraordinary thing, an action which is total.

You see, sirs, the earth is not communist or capitalist, it is not Hindu or Christian, it is neither yours nor mine. There is a feeling of the totality of the earth, of the beauty, the richness, the extraordinary potency of the earth; but you can feel that total splendor only when you are not committed to anything. In the same way, you can get the feeling of total action only when you are not committed to any particular activity, when you are not one of the "do-gooders" who are committed to this or that party, belief, or ideology, and whose actions are really a form of self-centered activity. If you are not committed, then you will find that the conscious mind, though involved with immediate action, can put aside that immediate action and inquire negatively into the unconscious where lie the real motives, the hidden contradictions, the traditional bondages and blind urges which create the problems of immediacy. And once you understand all this, then you can go much further. Then you will be able to feel—as you would feel the loveliness, the wholeness of a tree—the totality of action in which there is no opposite response, no contradiction.

New Delhi, 2nd Public Talk, February 11, 1959
Collected Works, Vol. XI, pp. 164-5

A human being is concerned with the total welfare, with the total misery, with the total confusion. And when we are clear on that issue, I think we can then ask: What is a human being to do?

I think there is a difference between a human being and an individual. The individual is a local entity, living in a particular country, belonging to a particular culture, a particular society, a particular religion, and so on. A human being is not a local entity, whether he is in America, in Russia, in China, or here. And I think we should bear that in mind while we are talking during these discussions. Then what is a human being to do? Because if the human being understands the totality of this problem and acts, then the individual has relationship to that totality. But if the individual merely acts in a particular corner of the vast field of life, then his activity is totally unrelated to the whole. So one has to bear in mind that we are talking of the whole and not of the part, of the whole of the human being—in Africa, in France, in Germany, here and elsewhere. Because in the greater is the lesser; but in the lesser the greater is not. And we are talking about the individual, and the individual is the little—conditioned, miserable, frustrated, endlessly discontented, satisfied with the little things, with his little gods, with his little traditions and so on. Whereas, a human being is concerned with the total welfare, with the total misery, with the total confusion. And when we are clear on that issue, I think we can then ask: What is a human being to do?

Seeing this enormous confusion, this revolt, this brutality, wars, the endless divisions of religion, nationalities, and so on—what is a human being to do when confronted with all this? I wonder if one has asked this question at all? Or, is one only concerned with one's own particular little problem—not that it is not important? But that problem, however little, however immediate, however urgent, relates to the whole existence of man. One cannot separate the individual's little problem from the totality of the human problems of life. And as all problems—the family problem, the social problem, the religious problem, the problem of poverty—are related, to concentrate on any one particular problem seems to me to be utterly meaningless.

So we have to consider man as a whole. And when he is faced with this tremendous challenge, not only outwardly but in his consciousness, the crisis is not only for the world outside the skin but also within the consciousness itself. The two really are not separate. I think it would be foolish to divide the world as the outer and the inner; they are both interrelated and therefore cannot be divided. But to understand this whole movement, this unitary process, one has objectively to understand not only the outward events, the various crises that we go through, but also the inward crises, the inward challenges within the field of consciousness. And when we are, as we are, faced with this issue, I am sure one must have asked, "What is this all about?"

This is rather a lovely evening—isn't it? The sun is on the leaves. There is a nice light on the leaves, and there is the gentle movement of the branches; and the light of the setting sun is coming through the leaves and through these woods. And somehow all that beauty is unrelated to our daily living; we pass it by, we are hardly aware of it; and if we are, we just glance at it and go on with our particular problem, our endless search about nothing! And we are incapable of looking either at that light on those leaves, or of hearing the birds, or of seeing clearly for ourselves non-fragmentarily, not in isolation, the totality of this issue of human existence. I hope you don't think I am becoming romantic when I look at those lights! But you know, without passion, without feeling, you cannot do anything in life. If you feel strongly about the poverty, the dirt, the squalor, the decay in this country, the corruption, the inefficiency, the appalling callousness that is going on round you, of which one is totally unaware; if you have a burning passion, an intensity about all that; and also if you have the passion to look at the flowers and the trees and the sun through the leaves, you will find that the two are not separate. If you cannot see that light on those leaves and take delight in it and be passionate in that delight, then I am afraid you will not be passionate in action either. Because action is necessary, not endless theories, endless discussions.

When you are confronted with this enormous and very complex problem of human discontent, human search, human longing for something beyond the structure of thought, you must have passion to find out. And passion is not put together by thought; passion is something new every minute. It is a living, vital, energizing thing; whereas thought is old, dead, something derived from the past. There is no new thought, for thought is the outcome of memory, experience, knowledge, which all belong to time, which is the past. And from the past, or by going to the past, there is no passion. You cannot revive a dead thing and be passionate about that dead thing.

Madras, 1st Public Talk, January 15, 1967
Collected Works, Vol. XVII, pp. 131-3

To understand this extraordinary movement of life—which is relationship, which is action—and to follow it right through endlessly, you must have freedom which comes alone when you give your mind, your heart, your whole being.

You know, when you love something—I am using that word in its total sense, not the love of God and the love of man, or profane love and love divine; those divisions are not love at all—you give your mind and your heart to it. This is not to commit yourself to something—which is entirely different. I can give my mind and heart and commit myself to some course of action—sociological or philosophical or communist or religious. That is not giving oneself, that is only an intellectual conviction, a sense of following something which you have to do to improve yourself or the society, and all the rest of it. But we are talking of something entirely different.

When you give your heart to something, then you are aware of everything in the sphere of that understanding. Do try some time—I hope you are doing it now as it is being said. The man who says, "I will try"—he is lost, because there is no time; there is only the moment now. And if you are doing it now, you will see that, if you give your heart, it is a total action—not a fragmentary, compulsive action, not the action according to some pattern or formula. When you give your heart, you will see that you understand that something immediately, instantly—which has nothing to do with sentiment or emotionalism or devotion; that is all too puerile. To give your heart to something you need tremendous understanding, you need great energy and clarity, so that in the light of clarity you see everything clearly. And you cannot see clearly if you are not free from your tradition, from your authority, from your culture, from your civilization, from all the patterns of society; it is not by escaping from society, going out into the mountains, or becoming a hermit, that you understand life. On the contrary, to understand this extraordinary movement of life—which is relationship, which is action—and to follow it right through endlessly, you must have freedom which comes alone when you give your mind, your heart, your whole being. Therefore in that state you understand. And when there is understanding, there is no effort; it is an instant act.

Madras, 1st Public Talk, December 16, 1964
Collected Works, Vol. XV, p. 6

What I am trying to convey is that there is an action in which idea is in no way involved, and therefore that action is direct and not the result of a mechanical memory. Such action releases tremendous energy, and you need tremendous energy to find out what is true, to discover what is beyond the measures which man has established for himself, beyond the things built by the mind.

Saanen, 9th Public Talk, July 25, 1963
Collected Works, Vol. XIII, p. 329

If the mind is capable of listening, that very listening brings about the good mind, from which action can come into being.

It seems to me very important to understand the quality of the mind, and to bring about that which is good. Most of us are not concerned with bringing about the good mind, but only with what to do. Action has become much more important than the quality of the mind. To me, action is secondary. If I may so put it, action does not matter, it is not important at all; because when there is the good mind, the mind that is creatively explosive, then from that creative explosiveness comes right action; it is not "doing is being," but "being is doing."

For most of us, action seems vital, important, and so we get caught in action; but the problem is not action, though it may appear to be. Most of us are concerned with how to live, what to do in certain circumstances, whether to take this side or that side in politics, and so on. If you observe you will see that our search is generally to find out what is the right action to take, and that is why there is anxiety, this pursuit of knowledge, this search for the guru. We inquire in order to find out what to do; and it seems to me that this approach to life must inevitably lead to a great deal of suffering and misery, to contradiction—not only within oneself but socially—a contradiction that invariably breeds frustration. To me, action inevitably follows being. That is, the very state of listening is an act of humility. If the mind is capable of listening, that very listening brings about the good mind, from which action can come into being. Whereas, without the good mind, without that strange, explosive quality of creativity, mere search for action leads to pettiness, to shallowness of heart and mind.

I do not know if you have noticed how most of us are occupied with what to do, and probably we have never had this quality of mind which immediately perceives the totality. The very perception of the totality is its own action, and I think it is important to understand this, because our culture has made us very shallow; we are imitative, traditionally bound, incapable of wide and deep vision, because our eyes are blinded by the immediate action and its results. Observe your own mind and you will see how concerned you are with what to do; and this constant occupation of the mind with what to do can only lead to very shallow thinking. Whereas, if the mind is concerned with the perception of the whole—not with how to perceive the whole, what method to use, which is again to be caught in the immediate action— then you will see that from this intention comes action, and not the other way around.

Bombay, 5th Public Talk, March 18, 1956
Collected Works, Vol. IX, p. 262

A. Seeing, perception, understanding, is action

Listening, as seeing, is acting.

So is it possible to see something so directly that that very seeing is the action, now? You are probably sitting in front of a tree, watching that tree. There is a distance between you and that tree—distance in time as well as in space. To go from where you are to that tree takes time: one second, two seconds. Therefore between you, the observer, and the thing observed, there is a time interval. Why does this time interval exist at all? It exists because you are looking at that tree with thought, with memory, with knowledge, with experience, with botanical information. So actually you are not looking at the tree, but the thought is looking at that tree. Right? So the relationship between you and the tree is the relationship of your image about that tree, and therefore you are not in contact with that tree at all. Only when you are in contact, you are in relationship; and you can only have that relationship when there is no image—which means no ideology, and therefore there is action.

* * * * *

So freedom is this action which springs immediately from seeing. Now, seeing is also listening—that is, to listen without the time interval. It is very simple if you know how to do it. And you must know. Otherwise your mind becomes stale, dull, caught and conditioned by an ideology, and therefore the mind can never be fresh, young, innocent, alive. As we said, as long as there is a time interval between the observer and the observed, that time interval creates friction and therefore it is a waste of energy; that energy is gathered to its highest point when the observer is the observed, in which there is no time interval. You hear that statement, but you have not listened to it. There is a difference between "hearing" and "listening." You can hear words, thinking you understand those words intellectually. Then you will ask, "How am I who have heard the words, to put those words into action?" You cannot put words into action! So you translate the words into thought, into an ideology, and then you have got the pattern and according to that pattern you are going to act. Now, listening is not to have that time interval at all. So listening, as seeing, is acting.

Madras, 2nd Public Talk, January 18, 1967
Collected Works, Vol. XVII, pp. 141-2

Action is not separate from understanding or perception or learning.

So this evening let us see if we cannot seriously, with full intent, put aside all that we know or think we know, all the things with which we are familiar, and look at the actual facts. Then, perhaps, we shall be able to learn; and learning is action. Action and learning are not separate. The movement of learning implies comprehension, seeing the significance of the problem—its width, its depth, its height. The very perception of the problem is action; action and perception are not separate. But when we have an idea about the problem, the idea is separate from action, and then the further problem arises of how to approximate action to the idea. So what matters is to look at the problem without fear, without anxiety, without our temperamental evaluations, for then we shall be able to learn; and that very movement of learning is action.

I think we should see this very clearly before we proceed; because we must act, we must bring about a tremendous revolution in our thinking, in our morality, in our relationships. There must obviously be a radical transformation, a total revolution in all the ways of our life. But we cannot be in that state of revolution if we do not see the fundamental fact that where there is understanding, there is action. Action is not separate from understanding or perception. When I understand a problem, that very understanding includes action. When I perceive deeply, that very perception brings an action of itself; but if I merely speculate, if I have an idea about the problem, then the idea is separate from action, and the further problem arises of how to carry out the idea. So let us bear very clearly in mind that understanding is action, that understanding is not separate from action.

New Delhi, 6th Public Talk, March 2, 1960
Collected Works, Vol. XI, p. 358

You can understand something only when you give your mind, your body, your senses, your eyes, your ears: everything. And out of that understanding is total action.

I mean by that word *understand* not something intellectual. A mind that is in fragmentation can never understand. When we say, "I understand something intellectually," what we really mean is we hear the word and understand the word—this is totally unrelated to understanding. Understanding implies not only the semantic nature and the meaning of the word but also the understanding of the whole content of that word and being totally aware of its significance as it applies to ourselves, completely. So understanding is not merely a matter of mentation, an intellectual process. You can understand something only when you give your mind, your body, your senses, your eyes, your ears: everything. And out of that understanding is total action, not a fragmentary, contradictory action.

Madras, 1st Public Talk, January 12, 1964
Collected Works, Vol. XIV, pp. 80-1

Out of that total comprehension alone is there action which does not bring about contradiction.

Life is action. These two are not separate. Life is not an idea carried out in action, just as you cannot have love as an idea. Love cannot be cultivated; it cannot be nurtured, produced; either there is love, or there is not. Similarly, there is understanding, or there is no understanding. To understand something one has to listen, and listening is an art. To listen to something implies that you are giving complete attention, not only to what the speaker is saying but also to those crows, to the sunset, to the clouds, to the breeze on the leaves, to the various colors that are here, so that your whole neurological system as well as the cells of the brain comprehend totally. Out of that total comprehension alone is there action which does not bring about contradiction and, therefore, conflict and endless pain and misery. So in that sense we are using the word *understanding*.

Madras, 4th Public Talk, December 27, 1964
Collected Works, Vol. XV, p. 20

All that you have to do is merely to watch. That is the greatest action. That is the only action.

KRISHNAMURTI: Before you understand what the state of mind is that understands, you have to go into the question of distraction. When you want to be concentrated on something, and your thought goes off, the going off is a distraction. I want to know why it goes off. That indicates that that particular thought has some interest. So the mind examines every thought, every wandering off; never saying it is a distraction. Therefore, such a mind is astonishingly awake, very intelligent, sharp, clear, because it is not in a battle with concentration and distraction. Therefore, it is watching everything.

Questioner: Is there anything to do after watching?

KRISHNAMURTI: All that you have to do is merely to watch. That is the greatest action. Out of that is action, and that is the only action.

Rajghat, Banaras, 2nd Public Talk, December 1, 1963
Collected Works, Vol. XIV, p. 66

B. Immediate, instantaneous action

Right through the world, there is a whole group of people, especially the young, who are saying that there must be action now, not tomorrow.

Is there an action in which time and ideology are not involved at all? That is: seeing is doing. That is what the world is demanding. The man who has nothing—no food, no clothes—who is tortured, is not going to wait for some evolutionary process to come into being, and for his being fed according to that ideology. He says, "Feed me now, not tomorrow." Right through the world, there is a whole group of people, especially the young, who are saying that there must be action now, not tomorrow. Now is much more important than tomorrow; the present generation is far more important than the generation to come.

So is there action without time and ideology? And that is the only revolution—which is, I see something as dangerous, and the very seeing is the acting. I see that nationalism—I am taking that as a very superficial example—is poison, because it divides people and so on. I see that as poison and drop the whole cultivation of nationalism completely and immediately. And immediacy of action is freedom.

Madras, 2nd Public Talk, January 18, 1967
Collected Works, Vol. XVII, p. 140

Revolt is never freedom. Freedom is something entirely different. And freedom comes only when you see and act, not through reaction. The seeing is the acting and, therefore, it is instantaneous: when you see danger, there is no mentation, there is no discussion, there is no hesitation; there is immediate action; the danger itself compels the act. And therefore, to see is to act and to be free. Therefore seeing is acting, and acting is the very essence of freedom—not revolt.

Madras, 1st Public Talk, January 15, 1967
Collected Works, Vol. XVII, p. 134

Questioner: Is immediate action total action?

KRISHNAMURTI: That is right, sir. I said, "immediate action." That is one of the most difficult things to understand; so don't just say, "immediate action." You know, there are people who say, "Live in the present." To live in the present is one of the most extraordinary things. To live in the present—which is the immediate action—one has to understand the conditioning, which is the past, and not project that past into the future; and one has therefore to eliminate the time interval and live in that extraordinary sense of the immediate.

Rajghat, Banaras, 3rd Public Talk, November 24, 1964
Collected Works, Vol. XIV, p. 295

Questioner: Is spontaneous action right action?

KRISHNAMURTI: Do you know how difficult it is to be really spontaneous? When we are so conditioned by society, when we live on memory, on the past, how can we possibly be spontaneous? Surely, to do something spontaneously is to act without motive, without calculation, without any self-interested feeling. It is not self-centered action. You just do it out of the fullness of your being. But to be really spontaneous requires stripping yourself completely of the past. It is only the innocent mind that can be spontaneous.

Saanen, 9th Public Talk, July 25, 1963
Collected Works, Vol. XIII, p. 332

You can live ten thousand years or ten days, or one day, or a split second more, but time will not resolve sorrow. So one has to learn immediately, not gradually...

For most people sorrow is self-pity, I have lost my son and I am left; and I am pitying myself that I have been left lonely, with nobody to help me fulfill—you know the whole business of self-pity. So is it possible to end that sorrow immediately, and not allow this habit of gradually getting rid of sorrow? That sorrow is not resolved by time; and we know that sorrow cannot be solved by time. You can live ten thousand years or ten days, or one day, or a split second more, but time will not resolve sorrow. So one has to learn immediately, not gradually, because there is no learning anything gradually—psychologically. If I learn a language, it will take time, many days, because I have to get used to the rhythm of the words, the sound of a strange word, the grammar, the syntax, how to put the words together, how to use the right word, the right verb, and so on. But here, if I allow time, sorrow will increase. So I have to learn about sorrow immediately, and the very act of learning is the complete cutting away of time. To see something immediately, to see the false immediately—that very seeing of the false is the action of truth, which frees you from time.

Rajghat, Banaras, 5th Public Talk, November 28, 1964
Collected Works, Vol. XIV, p. 306

Seeing the truth instantly is to act immediately.

Therefore, what is important is to see immediately the truth of something or the falseness of something. And you cannot see the truth or the falseness of something if you have an idea about it. Love is not an idea, love is instant action. When you bring an idea, when you have ideas about love—what it should be, what it should not be—then it ceases to be love; it is merely a process of thought. So this must be very clear before we proceed into what I am going to say: that it is possible to act without idea; which does not mean that action will be irrational, or that action will be postponed, or that action will be conditioned. That is, as long as ideas have supreme importance—for most of us they have—then action becomes irrelevant. Then we find that how to put those ideas into action becomes extraordinarily difficult.

So the question is: how to see the truth immediately? By "truth" I mean the truth of everyday living, everyday talk; the truth or the falseness of what you think, what you feel; to discover the truth of your motives, your daily activities, revealing your feeling instantly— the truth that is behind them. I am talking of that truth, not of the ultimate, because you cannot go to that extraordinary cause, the really immeasurable, without understanding the everyday truth of life— which is everyday activity, everyday thought. So you have to perceive the truth instantly, and not have ideas about what is truth; and seeing the truth instantly is to act immediately. If you see a snake you act immediately; there is not the idea first and then action; there is a danger, and your whole response to that danger is immediate; there is no interval of time which is idea. The response is instantaneous and that instantaneous response is real action.

New Delhi, 4th Public Talk, November 3, 1963
Collected Works, Vol. XIV, p. 21

When I realize the fact that I am conditioned, there is immediate action.

Now when you say, "I know I am conditioned," do you really know it, or is that merely a verbal statement? Do you know it with the same potency with which you see a cobra? When you see a snake and know it to be a cobra, there is immediate, unpremeditated action;

and when you say, "I know I am conditioned," has it the same vital significance as your perception of the cobra? Or is it merely a superficial acknowledgment of the fact, and not the realization of the fact? When I realize the fact that I am conditioned, there is immediate action. I don't have to make an effort to uncondition myself. The very fact that I am conditioned, and the realization of that fact, brings an immediate clarification.

New Delhi, 6th Public Talk, October 31, 1956
Collected Works, Vol. X, pp. 158-9

To give up something immediately, no time is involved at all.

I see that conflict cannot end through will. Will in itself breeds conflict. The very nature and structure of the will, to which we have become accustomed—the brain cells and all the rest of it—in their very structure breed conflict. I see very clearly that to live intensely, fully, completely, wholly, conflict is not necessary. Conflict, on the contrary, destroys. Will is gone, not verbally or theoretically, but actually; not as a hypothesis towards which I am working, which again becomes another conflict. Then what have I to do? How am I to give up without will, without fear? Smoking, sex or anything I take as an escape gives me pleasure, and becomes a habit, either pleasurable or painful. If it is painful it is easier to give it up, naturally. But a thing that gives pleasure, how am I to give it up without will, which means without time? If I say I'll give it up gradually, and day after day diminish the number of cigarettes I smoke, what has happened? There's a resistance all along.

Questioner: You have to understand why you smoke.

KRISHNAMURTI: We understand why we smoke. First of all, it's a habit. We did it as small boys and now it has become constant. We know why we smoke. It gives us something for us to do with our hands when we are with people, and we fiddle around. It's just that everyone does it, and we do it too. We are like a lot of monkeys, with our intense restlessness. Take drink, if you don't smoke. It's the same thing with drink, with sex, with any habit. Now please, sirs, this is very interesting. To give up smoking, sex, a particular habit of thinking, a particular way of living, a particular food, may be a very small affair, or a most complex affair. We see will is not the way out; and a gradual process is not the way out. It must be done instantly, without effort. To give up something immediately, no time is involved at all. How do we do it, sirs? I don't know why we make a mystery of it. It's very simple. There's a wasp there, a pretty large one. There it is. What takes place when we see it? There is immediate action to get away from it.

Questioner: There is fear.

KRISHNAMURTI: Please don't reduce it so quickly; just look at it; look at it. There is a wasp. You know that it stings, causes pain. There is an immediate reaction: to kill it, to run away from it, or to push it out. It is a physiological reaction; it is not an intellectual process. It may have been at the beginning, but now it is a physical reaction. There is instant movement, instant action. Your brain cells, your nerves, your whole being responds, because there is a danger. If you don't respond, there's something wrong with your nerves, with your brain, with your whole nervous organism. You have to respond. So there is a state when you can respond immediately. When you see danger, physical danger, you respond instantly, the body responds before the mind enters. I once saw a tiger in the wilderness; there was immediate reaction, and that reaction is necessary. It is a healthy reaction, and it is instant.

Rome, 2nd Public Discussion, April 3, 1966
Collected Works, Vol. XVI, pp. 97-8

So a mind that chooses is always in conflict. But a mind that sees what is true acts instantly on that perception; it is not in conflict.

What is involved in a decision? I decide to do this and not that; that has already created a conflict. But when you see the truth of this and the truth of that—either the truth of this and the falseness of that, or the falseness of this and the truth of that—when you see the truth, that seeing will act; it is not a decision.

Therefore do not decide, don't choose; then there is no conflict. See what is true—that requires astonishing intelligence. You cannot see what is true when you take what Sankara or any other person has said as true, and follow him.

So a mind that chooses is always in conflict. But a mind that sees what is true acts instantly on that perception; it is not in conflict. Such action is the only action.

Rajghat, Banaras, 1st Public Talk, November 24, 1963
Collected Works, Vol. XIV, pp. 55-6

If the mind does see the fact, without translating it in terms of the old, then there is immediate perception.

So can we realize inwardly, see the actual fact that all our action is reaction, all our action is born from the motive to achieve, to arrive, to become something, to get somewhere? Can I just realize that fact, without introducing the "what shall I do," "what about the family, my job," and all that? Because, if the mind does see the fact, without translating it in terms of the old, then there is immediate perception; then one will understand that action which is not a reaction; and that understanding is an essential quality of the new mind.

London, 2nd Public Talk, May 4, 1961
Collected Works, Vol. XII, p. 128

C. Complete attention

Do you know for yourself the quality of this attention, the feeling of a mind which is not compelled to concentrate, which has no object to gain and is therefore capable of attention without motive?

Do you know a total action at any time in your life? And what do we mean by a total action? Surely, there is a total action only when your whole being—your mind, your heart, your body—is in it completely, without division or separation. And when does that happen? Please, sirs, go with me slowly. When does such a thing take place?

Total action takes place only when there is complete attention, does it not? And what do we mean by complete attention?

Please, I am thinking this out as I go along, I am not repeating it from memory. I am watching, learning. Similarly, you must watch your own mind, and not just listen to my verbal explanations. What do we mean by attention? When the mind concentrates on an object, is that attention? When the mind says, "I must look at this one thing and eliminate all other thoughts," is that attention? Or is it a process of exclusion, and therefore not attention? In attention, surely, there is no effort, there is no object to be concentrated upon. The moment you have an object upon which you concentrate, that object becomes more important than attention. The object is then merely a means of absorbing your mind; your mind is absorbed by an idea, as a child is absorbed by a toy, and in that process there is no attention because there is exclusion.

Nor is there attention when there is a motive, obviously. It is only when there is no motive, when there is no object, when there is no compulsion in any form, that there is attention. And do you know such attention? Not that you must experience it, or learn about it from me; but do you know for yourself the quality of this attention, the feeling of a mind which is not compelled to concentrate, which has no object to gain and is therefore capable of attention without motive? Do you understand, sirs? What is important is not how to get it, but actually to feel the quality of complete attention as you are listening to me.

Now when does complete attention take place? Surely, only when there is love. When there is love there is complete attention. There is no need of a motive, there is no need of an object, there is no need of compulsion: you just love. It is only when there is love that there is complete attention, and therefore total action in response to political, religious, and social problems. But we have no love; nor are the political leaders, the social and religious reformers concerned with love. If they were, they would not talk of mere reform, nor create new patterns of thought. Love is not sentimentality, it is not emotionalism, it is not devotion. It is a state of being: clear, sane, rational, uncorrupted, out of which comes the total action which alone can give the true reply to all our problems.

Madras, 2nd Public Talk, December 16, 1956
Collected Works, Vol. X, p. 175

Concentration narrows down all thought to a certain point and so is an exclusive process. So invariably our action, being born of concentration, is limited.

I think there is a difference between concentration and attention. Attention is awareness of the whole field of thought; attention is extensive; it has, if you observe, no frontier, no limitation. Attention is an awareness of the whole, and in that state, when you give attention to any problem, then you are able to observe the whole field of thought and also comprehend the implications and significance of the problem. Whereas concentration narrows down all thought to a certain point and so is an exclusive process. So invariably our action, being born of concentration, is limited; and in that state of concentration there is no attention. But when there is attention—in that extensive sense of the mind being without a frontier—there can also be concentration. The little does not hold the big, but the big can hold the little.

Bombay, 4th Public Talk, December 7, 1958
Collected Works, Vol. XI, p. 119

If you are attentive, attentive to everything that is going on about you…then out of that attention you can know a different kind of concentration.

You know what it is to give attention to something. Attention is not concentration. When you concentrate, as most people try to do—what takes place when you are concentrating? You are cutting yourself off, resisting, pushing away every thought except that one particular thought, that one particular action. So your concentration breeds resistance, and therefore concentration does not bring freedom. Please, this is very simple if you observe it yourself. But whereas if you are attentive, attentive to everything that is going on about you, attentive to the dirt, the filth of the street, attentive to the bus which is so dirty; attentive [to] your words, your gestures, the way you talk to your boss, the way you talk to your servant, to the superior, to the inferior; the respect, the callousness to those below you, the words, the ideas—if you are attentive to all that, not correcting, then out of that attention you can know a different kind of concentration. You are then aware of the setting, the noise of the people, people talking over there on the roof, your hushing them up, asking them not to talk, turning your head, you are aware of the various colors, the costumes; and yet concentration is going on. Such concentration is not exclusive, in that there is no effort, whereas mere [ordinary] concentration demands effort. So if you give your attention totally—that is, with your nerves, with your eyes, with your ears, with your mind, with your brain, totally, completely—to understand fear, then you will see you can instantly be free of it, completely. Because it is only a very clear mind, not living in the darkness of fear, or in the confusion of many wants— it is only such a clear, lucid mind that can go beyond death, because it has understood living. Living is not a battle, is not a torture; living is not something to be run away from to the mountains, to the monastery. We run away because living [has become for us] a torture, an ugly nightmare. If you give your attention to one thing totally, out of that freedom you will see, you will know, what love is.

New Delhi, 4th Public Talk, November 18, 1965
Collected Works, Vol. XV, p. 321

What is important is not what we are doing but whether we can give total attention.

Questioner: I feel that my daily life is unimportant, that I should be doing something else.

KRISHNAMURTI: When you are eating, eat. When you are going for a walk, walk. Don't say, "I [should] be doing something else." When you are reading, give your attention completely to that, whether it is a detective novel, a magazine, the Bible, or what you will. The complete attention is a complete action, and therefore there is no "I must be doing something else." It is only when we are inattentive that we have the feeling of "By Jove, I must be doing something better." If we give complete attention when we are eating, that is action. What is important is not what we are doing but whether we can give total attention. I mean by that word, not something we learn through concentration in a school or in business, but to attend—with our bodies, our nerves, our eyes, our ears, our minds, our hearts—completely. If we do that there is a tremendous crisis in our lives. Then something demands our whole energy, vitality, attention. Life demands that attention every minute, but we are so trained to inattention that we are always trying to escape from attention to inattention. We say, "How am I to attend? I am lazy." Be lazy, but be totally attentive to the laziness. Be totally attentive to inattention. Know that you are completely inattentive. Then when you know that you are totally attentive to inattention, you are attentive.

Saanen, 9th Public Talk, July 28, 1966
Collected Works, Vol. XVI, p. 246

When you are inattentive, don't act...because it's inattention that breeds mischief and misery.

KRISHNAMURTI: When you are completely attentive, giving your mind, your heart, your nerves, your eyes, your ears, when everything is attentive, there is no time at all. You then don't say, "Well, I was attentive yesterday, and I'm not today." Attention is not a continuous momentum of time. Either you are attentive, or you are not attentive. Most of us are inattentive, and in that state of inattention we act and create misery for ourselves. If you are totally attentive to what is taking place in the world—the starvation, the wars, the disease—the whole, then the division of man against man comes to an end.

Questioner: There are moments almost like that, but the next day or the next moment it's gone. How am I to keep that memory which I have had?

KRISHNAMURTI: It's a memory, and therefore it's a dead thing. Therefore it's not awareness, not attention. Attention is completely in the present. That's the art of living, sir. When you are inattentive, don't act. That requires a great deal of intelligence, a great deal of self-observation; because it's inattention that breeds mischief and misery. When you are completely attentive with all your being, in that state action is instantaneous. But the mind remembers that action and wants to repeat it, and then you are lost.

Questioner: Can you speak about the relation of action, energy, and attention?

KRISHNAMURTI: I am doing it, sir. Inattention is a dissipation of energy. And we are trained, through education, through all the social and psychological structure of the world to be inattentive. People think for us—they tell us what to do, what to believe, they tell us how to experience, to use a new drug—and we, like sheep, follow. All that is inattention. When there is self-knowledge, when there is delving deeply into the whole structure, the nature of oneself, then attention becomes a natural thing. There is great beauty in attention.

New York, 3rd Public Talk, September 30, 1966
Collected Works, Vol. XVII, pp. 22-3

D. The miracle of listening

Once [you] understand this extraordinary act of listening, then you will see that [that] action is totally different from the action that is derived from an idea.

I would like to point out how important it is to listen, because most of us hardly ever listen to anything. To listen properly without projecting your own particular prejudices, idiosyncrasies, and all that you have learned, is very difficult—to listen with intense curiosity as though you are for the first time learning, for the first time inquiring, and as though the whole field is open to you; and to go step by step into it without any conclusion, without any memory, inquiring, moving, running, seeing, finding out. Such an act of listening needs attention—not the attention of concentration, not the attention that you give when you are seeking profit or when you want something—and you listen without wanting, without seeking, but merely inquiring. And to inquire really deeply, you need freedom, and the act of listening is freedom. Once [you] understand this extraordinary act of listening or seeing immediately, comprehending something instantly, then you will see that [that] action is totally different from the action that is derived with an idea or from an idea.

New Delhi, 4th Public Talk, November 3, 1963
Collected Works, Vol. XIV, p. 20

In the very act of listening, the nature of action is changed.

So I would like to talk about listening, because it seems to me that in listening there is no effort at all. There is effort only if you don't understand the language, the words that are being used. When you try to listen, try to follow what the speaker is saying; when you try to concentrate, to put your whole mind on it, it prevents you from listening. Listening implies no inward contradiction; there is no attempt to do something, no endeavor to capture or to realize something; you just listen, easily, with an attention that doesn't demand concentration. And what I am going to talk about needs very deep listening—not just hearing through the ears, but listening with an extraordinary profundity. If you can listen in this way, you will find that you have understood for yourself a great many things; and in the very act of listening, the nature of action is changed. Because listening is an action; it isn't something apart from daily activity. It includes listening to your wife or husband, to your children, to your neighbor, to noises, to all the ugly things that go on in life, to all the brutalities, the words of cruelty, to the words of pleasure and pain. And you will find that in this act of listening a mutation is taking place in the very nature of action itself.

Saanen, 5th Public Talk, July 16, 1963
Collected Works, Vol. XIII, pp. 301-2

Ideas are not at all important...but what is important is how you listen...

If you know how to listen, then that very listening is a complete action in itself. I think it is important to understand this, if I may labor the point, because I am not giving out new ideas. Ideas are not at all important. One may have new ideas, or you may listen to something which you have not heard before; but what is important is how you listen, not only to ideas, to something new, but to everything, because if you know how to listen, that very act of listening is a liberation.

New York, 1st Public Talk, May 22, 1954
Collected Works, Vol. VIII, p. 213

Really, if you know how to listen, the miracle takes place. If you can listen to the pure sound, to the silence between two notes, then perhaps you will find out the truth of anything. But as long as you are comparing, rejecting, accepting with the constant activity of explanation and rejection, you are not actually listening.

Poona, India, 4th Public Talk, February 1, 1953
Collected Works, Vol. VII, p. 167

We have never listened to ourselves—listened with care so that everything, every detail is revealed.

We have never listened to ourselves. We know we have only said to ourselves, "I must," "I must not," "This is right," "This is wrong," "This is good," "This is bad," "I must conform to this," "I must do this," or "I must not do this." That is [all that] we have said. We have never listened to ourselves—listened with care so that everything, every detail is revealed. And that is the beginning of self-knowing. Without self-knowing, you have no basis for any action, because then all action leads to misery, to despair.

Bombay, 1st Public Talk, February 9, 1964
Collected Works, Vol. XIV, p. 127

When you are so completely listening, there is no idea; there is only a state of listening.

Please, for this evening, if I may suggest, just listen. Don't accept or deny; don't build defenses so as to prevent listening, by having your own thoughts, beliefs, contradictions and all that. But just listen. We are not trying to convince you of anything; we are not forcing you through any means to conform to a particular idea, or pattern, or action. We are merely stating facts, whether you like them or not; and what is important is to learn about the fact. "Learning" implies total listening, a complete observation. When you listen to the sound of the crow, do not listen with your own noises, with your own fears, thoughts, with your own ideas, with your own opinions. Then you will see that there is no idea at all, but you are actually listening.

So in the same way, this evening, if I may suggest, just listen. Just listen, not only consciously but also unconsciously—which is perhaps much more important. Most of us are influenced. We can reject conscious influences, but it is much more difficult to put aside the unconscious influences. When you are listening in the manner of which we have talked, then it is neither conscious nor unconscious listening. Then you are completely attentive. And attention is not yours or mine; it is not nationalistic; it is not religious; it is not divisible. Hence, when you are so completely listening, there is no idea; there is only a state of listening. Most of us do this when we are listening to something rather beautiful—when there is lovely music, or when you are seeing a mountain, the light of the evening, or the light on the water, or a cloud—then in that state of attention, in that state of listening, seeing, there is no idea.

Bombay, 7th Public Talk, March 3, 1965
Collected Works, Vol. XV, p. 89

If I know how to listen...then that very listening brings about an extraordinary activity which is not a conscious endeavor on my part.

If you can listen rightly, without interpreting or comparing what you have already read about or heard, listen as though you were enjoying yourself, and try to find out, to inquire, not to block, not to hinder, but to really find out—which is entirely different from hearing lectures. We are used to going to talks. We hear lots of speeches made up of words, very brilliant or crudely put together. But the effect of true listening is much more revolutionary than that particular action. If I know how to listen to you, to music, to the sound of a wave, if I know how to listen to it, if I let it penetrate into me without any barrier, then that very listening brings about an extraordinary activity which is not a conscious endeavor on my part.

Bombay, 3rd Public Talk, February 15, 1953
Collected Works, Vol. VII, p. 189

And if you do listen in that happy manner, with an ease, without any strain, then that very act of listening is a miracle. It is a miracle because in that action, in that moment, you comprehend all the act of listening, understanding, seeing; and you have broken down the walls, and there is space between you and the world and the thing you are listening to. And you must have this space, to observe, to see, to listen. The wider, the deeper that space, the more beauty, the more depth there is.

Madras, 4th Public Talk, January 22, 1964
Collected Works, Vol. XIV, pp. 96-7

It [listening] is a total act, not a partial act. And if we could listen that way all our life…then life would become an endless action of learning and listening.

The act of listening is always in the present. It is a movement always in the present. And the moment you translate what you hear in terms of your own understanding, of your own tradition, of your own culture—if you have a culture—you merely prevent listening. If one is listening, then one can go on in an extraordinary movement endlessly, not only listening to the speaker, but listening to everything: to those crows, to that bus, listening to the movement of the breeze among the leaves, seeing the sunset. It is a total act, it is not a partial act. And if we could listen that way all our life, not just for a few minutes but right through our life, listening to every sound, not only to the sound of a voice with which one is familiar but also to every movement of thought and word, then life would become an endless action of learning and listening.

Madras, 6th Public Talk, January 3, 1965
Collected Works, Vol. XV, p. 34

E. Love

If you know yourself, you will know what it means to love, and out of that there is total action, which is the only good action.

It is because you have no love that you pretend to change; on the circumference you reform, but the core is empty. You will know how to act totally only when you know what it means to love.

Sirs, we have developed our minds, we are so-called intellectuals, which means that we are full of words, explanations, techniques. We are disputatious, clever at arguing, at opposing one opinion with another. We have filled our hearts with the things of the mind, and that is why we are in a state of contradiction. But love is not easily come by; you have to work hard for it. Love is difficult to understand— difficult in the sense that to understand it you have to know where reason is necessary and go with reason as far as possible, and also know its limitations. This means that to understand what it is to love, there must be self- knowledge—not the knowledge of Shankara, Buddha, or Christ, which you gather from books. Such books are just books, they are not divine revelations. The divine revelation comes into being only through self-knowledge; and you can know yourself, not according to the pattern of some psychologist, but only by observing how your thought is functioning, that is, by watching yourself from moment to moment as you get into the bus, as you talk to your children, to your wife, to your servant.

So if you know yourself, you will know what it means to love, and out of that there is total action, which is the only good action. No other action is good, however clever, however profitable, however reformatory. But to love, you need immense humility—which is just to be humble, not to cultivate humility. To be humble is to be sensitive to everything about you, not only to the beautiful, but also to the ugly; it is to be sensitive to the stars, to the stillness of an evening, to the trees, to the children, to the dirty village, to the servant, to the politician, to the tramcar driver. Then you will see that your sensitivity, which is love, has an answer to the many problems of life, because love is the answer to all the problems which the mind creates.

Love is to be found directly by each one of us, and not at the feet of a guru, or through any book. Love must be found alone, because it is uncontaminated, pure, and you must come to it completely stripped of greed, of envy, and all the stupidities of society which have made the mind limited, small, petty. Then there is a total action, and that total action is the answer to man's problems, not the separate activities of the reformer, the planner, and the politician.

Madras, 2nd Public Talk, December 16, 1956
Collected Works, Vol. X, pp. 175-6

We cannot hope to resolve the basic human problem by reforming and putting together again its many parts.

It seems to me that only love can produce the right revolution, and that every other form of revolution—that is, revolution based on economic theories, on social ideologies, and so on—can only bring about further disorder, more confusion and misery. We cannot hope to resolve the basic human problem by reforming and putting together again its many parts. It is only when there is great love that we can have a total outlook and therefore a total action, instead of this partial, fragmentary activity which we now call revolution, and which leads nowhere.

Saanen, 8th Public Talk, July 28, 1964
Collected Works, Vol. XIV, pp. 208-9

Love is something in action, immediately. And when you bring an idea, it is no longer love.

Now, we mean by revolution something that is not an idea separated from action. It is not a planned revolution. The very term *planned revolution* is contradictory in itself. It has no meaning. A planned revolution is merely conforming to a pattern established by another, whoever it is. That is not a revolution; it is only an action based on an idea formulated according to a certain pattern—which is a reaction according to which you must act. You approximate your action according to that reaction, and therefore it ceases to be action; there, the idea is more important than action—than to do, to act, to function. The revolution of which we are talking is not an idea carried out in action;

therefore, in the action brought about by this revolution, there is no conflict, no approximation, no imitation of an idea. Please do see this. Perhaps it is something new which you have not read or heard, and therefore you are a little bit bewildered, and you say, "How can you act without an idea?"

You know what love is? Love is not an idea. Love is not a formula according to which you live. Love is not a concept according to which you approximate your action. Love is something in action, immediately. And when you bring an idea, it is no longer love. We have an idea of what love should be. Therefore we have stopped, we have ceased to love. We know the idea of what love should be: it must be chaste, it must be non-physical, it must be divine, it must be this, it must be that. All such ideas are established in words, in patterns, in formulas; and we do not know what it means to love, to care, to have real feeling for people, for things, for trees, for animals...

The saints have told you that to find God you must renounce, you must have no sexual relationship, you must not look, you must not have feelings, you must suppress, you must subjugate, you must destroy. What happens when you sit on a feeling? It pops up in another direction. You are boiling inside and you suppress; you say, "In order to find God, I must live a bachelor's life," and so you go round and round in a circle, never finding God and never understanding the whole problem. So idea and action create real hell in our lives, real misery in our lives, when we separate the two.

Is it possible to act without idea? It is possible. And it is only possible when you observe without conflict, and therefore there is action instantly. And that action is not conformity. That action is an extraordinary releasing process, and therefore that action is revolutionary.

New Delhi, 7th Public Talk, November 13, 1963
Collected Works, Vol. XIV, pp. 44-5

Questioner: Will you please go into learning while acting?

KRISHNAMURTI: They have found in certain factories that if a man keeps on repeating work in the same way, doing the same thing, he produces less because he gets bored with doing the same repetitive thing, but if he is allowed to learn as he is doing, he produces more. That is what they are discovering; so they let the worker learn as he is doing.

Look at it the other way. Most of us have ideas. To us ideas, formulas, concepts are tremendously important. Nationality is an idea. The negro, the Hindu, the white are ideas. Though those ideas have produced certain terrible activities, for us ideas, ideologies, formulas are tremendously important, but action is not important. We act according to those concepts, those ideas; we approximate action to the idea. There is always a division between the idea and the act, and therefore there is always a conflict. A man who would understand and end conflict has to understand whether he can act without idea; he must be learning as he is acting.

Let us take love. It is not a simple thing; it is quite complex. We do not know what love means. We have ideas about it, that we must be jealous to love, that love is divided into divine and human. We have many ideas. To find out what it means, the depth of it, the beauty of it, whether there is such a thing as love—which has nothing to do with good works, with sympathy, with tolerance, with gentleness, although all those may be included in it. If I really want to find out, I must throw away all my ideas about it, and in the throwing away of all my concepts about love, I am learning about it. That is all.

Saanen, 4th Public Talk, July 17, 1966
Collected Works, Vol. XVI, pp. 218-9

The action of love has no motive, and every other action has.

When the mind realizes the totality of its own conditioning— which it cannot do as long as it is merely pursuing its own comfort, or lazily taking the easy course—then all its movements come to an end; it is completely still, without any desire, without any compulsion, without any motive. Only then is there freedom.

"But we have to live in this world, and whatever we do, from earning a livelihood to the most subtle inquiry of the mind, has some motive or other. Is there ever action without motive?"

Don't you think there is? The action of love has no motive, and every other action has.

Commentaries On Living, Series III, p. 60

When you love something with your whole being, there is no self-contradiction.

Self-contradiction is not productive of intelligence, but only of cunning. It produces a certain efficiency in adjusting oneself to the environment—and that is what most of us are doing. Self-contradiction, with its ceaseless effort, places a bondage on consciousness; and action born of self-contradiction is fundamentally productive of misery, though on the surface it may seem to be worthwhile. If your mind is in a state of self-contradiction, you may do good superficially, but essentially you are creating further misery. Of course, the streets must be cleaned, and all the rest of it—but we are not talking about that.

* * * * *

Sirs, when you love something with your whole being, there is no self-contradiction. But most of us have not that wholeness of love. Our love is divided as carnal and spiritual, sacred and profane, and all the rest of that nonsense. We do not know the love which is a total feeling, a completeness of being, which is neither of the past nor of the future, and which is not concerned with its own continuity. That feeling is total, it has no border, no frontier, and that feeling is action free of self-contradiction. Don't say, "How am I to get it?" It is not an ideal, a thing to be gained, a goal you must arrive at. If it is an ideal, throw it out, because it will only create greater contradiction in your life. You have enough ideals, enough miseries—don't add another. We are talking about something entirely different: freeing the mind of all ideals, and therefore of all contradiction. If you see the truth of that, it is enough.

Bombay, 2nd Public Talk, December 27, 1959
Collected Works, Vol. XI, p. 264

Love can only come into being when there is this passion of feeling. Then out of that feeling there is action...

Religion, after all, is the discovery of love, and love is something to be discovered from moment to moment. You must die to the love that you have known a second before, in order to ever know anew what love is. And love can only come into being when there is this passion of feeling. Then, out of that feeling there is action, and that action will not bind you because love never binds. And so religion is not the thing that we have now, which is a miserable thing, a dark thing, a deadly thing. Religion implies clarity, light, passion; it implies a mind that is empty and therefore able to receive that immeasurable, incorruptible richness.

Bombay, 9th Public Talk, December 24, 1958
Collected Works, Vol. XI, p. 148

F. Action, silence, and the religious mind

We can help each other to find the door to reality, but each one must open that door for himself; and this, it seems to me, is the only positive action.

It is only when the mind is no longer acquisitive, no longer seeking or demanding anything, that it is free to find out what is true, what is God.

That is why it is very important to understand ourselves—not analytically, with one part of the mind analyzing another part, which merely leads to further confusion, but actually to be aware, without judgment or condemnation, of the way we act, the words we use, of all our various emotions, our hidden thoughts. If we can look at ourselves dispassionately, so that the hidden emotions are not pressed back but invited forth and understood, then the mind becomes really quiet; and only then there is the possibility of leading a full life.

These are the things which I think we should explore together. We can help each other to find the door to reality, but each one must open that door for himself; and this, it seems to me, is the only positive action.

So there must be in each one of us an inward, religious revolution; for it is only this inward, religious revolution which will totally change the way of our thinking. And to bring about this revolution, there must be the silent observation of the responses of the mind, without judgment, condemnation, or comparison. At present the mind is uncreative, in the true sense of that word, is it not? It is a made-up thing, put together through the accumulations of memory. As long as there is envy, ambition, self-seeking, there can be no creativeness. So it seems to me that all we can do is to understand ourselves, the ways of our own mind; and this process of understanding is an enormous task. It is not to be done casually, later on, tomorrow, but rather every day, every moment, all the time. To understand ourselves is to be aware spontaneously, naturally, of the ways of our own thinking, so that we begin to see all the hidden motives and intentions which lie behind our thoughts, and thereby bring about the liberation of the mind from its own binding and limiting processes. Then the mind is still; and in that stillness something which is not of the mind can come into being of its own accord.

Stockholm, 1st Public Talk, May 14, 1956
Collected Works, Vol. X, pp. 3-4

Can I look without the word at every problem...?

I can look at a flower, a cloud or a bird on the wing without a center, without a word, the word which creates thought. Can I look without the word at every problem—the problem of fear, the problem of pleasure? Because the word creates, breeds thought; and thought is memory, experience, pleasure, and therefore a distorting factor.

This is really quite astonishingly simple. Because it is simple, we mistrust it. We want everything to be very complicated, very cunning; and all cunning is covered with a perfume of words. If I can look at a flower non verbally—and I can; anyone can do it, if one gives sufficient attention—can't I look with that same objective, non-verbal attention at the problems which I have? Can't I look out of silence, which is non-verbal, without the thinking machinery of pleasure and time being in operation? Can't I just look? I think that's the crux of the whole matter, not to approach from the periphery, which only complicates life tremendously, but to look at life, with all its complex problems of livelihood, sex, death, misery, sorrow, the agony of being tremendously alone—to look at all that without association, out of silence, which means without a center, without the word which creates the reaction of thought, which is memory and hence time. I think that is the real problem, the real issue: whether the mind can look at life where there is immediate action, not an idea and then action, and eliminate conflict altogether.

London, 6th Public Dialogue, May 9, 1965
Collected Works, Vol. XV, p. 143

When there is silence, out of that silence, there is action; and that action is never complicated, never confused, never contradictory.

So silence comes because there is aloneness. And that silence is beyond consciousness. Consciousness is pleasure, thought, and the machinery of all that, conscious or unconscious; in that field there can never be silence; and therefore in that field any action will always bring confusion, will always bring sorrow, will always create misery.

It is only when there is action out of this silence that sorrow ends. Unless the mind is completely free from sorrow—personal or otherwise—it lives in darkness, in fear and in anxiety, and therefore, whatever its action, there will always be confusion, and whatever its choice, it will always bring conflict. So when one understands all that, there is silence, and where there is silence, there is action. Silence itself is action—not silence and then action. Probably this has never happened to you—to be completely silent. If you are silent, you can speak out of that silence though you have your memories, experiences, knowledge. If you had no knowledge, you would not be able to speak at all! But when there is silence, out of that silence, there is action; and that action is never complicated, never confused, never contradictory.

Madras, 6th Public Talk, January 9, 1966
Collected Works, Vol. XVI, pp. 38-9

The religious man moves from the outward to the inward like a tide, so that there is a perfect balance and a sense of integration, not with the outer and the inner as two separate movements but as a unitary movement.

I think it would be a great mistake if we treat these talks as a theoretical affair, approximating our lives to ideas or ideals. That surely is not what we are doing. We are moving very carefully and advisedly from fact to fact, which is after all the approach of a scientist. The scientist may have various theories, but he pushes those aside when he is confronted with facts; he is concerned with the observation of outward things, the things that are about matter, whether it is near or far; to him there is only matter and the observation of that matter—the outward movement. The religious mind is concerned with the fact and moving from the fact; and its outward movement is a unitary process with its inward movement—the two movements are not separate. The religious man moves from the outward to the inward like a tide; and there is this constant movement from the outer to the inner and from the inner to the outer, so that there is a perfect balance and a sense of integration, not with the outer and the inner as two separate movements but as a unitary movement.

If one observes very carefully, one sees what an extraordinary thing anonymity is. The anonymous approach after all is required to understand a fact. To see the reality of what is false or to find out what is truth, there must be the approach of the anonymous, not the approach of tradition, of hope, of despair, of an idea—which are all identified with something or other, and therefore can never be anonymous. A monk who withdraws into a monastery and takes a name is not anonymous, nor the sannyasi, because they are still identified with their conditioning. One has really to be aware of this extraordinary movement of the outer and the inner as a unitary process, and the understanding of this whole thing must be anonymous. Therefore it is very important to understand all conditioning and to be aware of that conditioning, and to shatter through that.

I hope you are aware of the significance of listening. You are not merely listening to me, to the speaker; but you are also at the same time listening to your own mind—the mind is listening to itself—because what is being said is merely an indication. But what is more important is that through this indication one begins to listen—the mind begins to listen to itself, and is aware of itself, aware of every movement of thought. Then I think these talks would be of significance and worthwhile. But if you merely treat them as a theory, something to be thought over, and after thinking over, to come to a conclusion, and then approximating your daily life with that conclusion, these talks would seem to be utterly futile. When there is a condemnatory process or justification, there is an identification with thought. One has to see the significance of all this as we go along. We have been talking about the religious mind and the scientific mind. Every other mind is a mischievous mind, whether it is of a learned person or of a very erudite person or of the sannyasi who has given up this and that; the political mind is, of course, the most destructive mind. The real scientific mind observes, analyzes, dissects, goes into the outward movement of life without any compromise; the scientist may compromise outside the laboratory where he is still a conditioned human being; but inside the laboratory there is that spirit of inquiry and research as a ruthless pursuit of fact; that is the only spirit in the scientific field, and our minds must be that, to understand. The mind must also have this comprehension of the outer as well as the inner; and as these are the only two actual facts, one begins to understand these two as a unitary process; and it is only the religious mind that can comprehend the unitary process. Then whatever action springs from the religious mind—that is the action that will not bring about misery, confusion.

Bombay, 7th Public Talk, March 5, 1961
Collected Works, Vol. XII, pp. 89-90

A mind that is completely empty—empty in the sense of observation, silence, and therefore, love, and the whole understanding of death—such a mind is creative...And it is only such a religious mind that can solve the problems of misery in this world.

Have you ever wondered how the scientists have extraordinary energy? When you go into a laboratory, if you have ever gone into a first-class research laboratory, there you will see the scientist completely full of energy, active. Because he is dealing with outward things, there is no resistance; he is moving from fact to fact; he does not indulge in theories, hypotheses, speculations; he is not a theoretician. He is a pure, clear-sighted technician, watching everything under the

87

microscope. Therefore he has tremendous energy there in the laboratory. But let him go outside, he is just like everybody else: anxious,
fighting for position, competing, nationalistic, caught in religious beliefs, or inventing his own particular belief, and so on. There is a waste
of energy.

And to look, the mind must be completely silent. After all, if the
scientist is looking through the microscope, or whatever he is doing,
he is observing from silence, not from knowledge. What he sees, he
then translates in terms of knowledge, and therefore there is action.
But he sees from silence—it may be that silence may last a split second or an hour. And that is the only way to observe.

So the cultivation of a silent mind becomes stupid. You cannot
practice and arrive at a silent mind. But to look, to observe, you must
have silence. Do look at that sunset. You cannot look at that sunset,
you cannot see it, if your mind is chattering. You can see it completely
only when the mind is extraordinarily quiet and intense. After all, that
is beauty. That is, the perception of beauty or non-beauty is only possible when there is passion, when you look at that sunset with complete intensity. And you cannot be intense if you are not silent. So you
begin to see how extraordinarily silent the mind becomes when you
observe. When you are observing, you do not have to discipline the
mind to be silent—then it is a dead mind. But the mind that is observing out of silence creates its own discipline; it does not need discipline
because it is observing.

This observation out of silence is passion, is energy. Then you
can observe your fears. Most people are frightened—frightened of
death, frightened of this empty, useless life. And one has to meet that
fear, and to observe it without any movement, without trying to go
beyond it or to resist it, without trying to get rid of it. To go beyond it,
to overcome it, to suppress it—these are [a] waste of energy. Whereas
if you observe the whole movement of fear, then that observation out
of silence gives energy; then that problem of fear ceases.

* * * * *

So there has to be this observation of daily events. When we are
using the word *observation*, we mean the observation which is not
critical, which is not the outcome of discontent or conformity or suppression, but which is the observation out of silence, the observation
of fact only, not the translation of that fact or the opinion about the

fact. Then you will see, out of this observation, there is no effort necessary to do, to resist, to overcome or to deny, effort altogether goes away. And one can live one's daily life—going to an office, cooking, doing everything—without effort.

The religious mind is the mind that understands the family and its position relative to the whole; the mind that does not seek power, position; the mind that is not caught in any ritual, any dogma, any belief, any organized church or temple; the mind that has no power whatsoever to create illusion. And the religious mind is the mind that looks at facts, and therefore does not make any effort at all whatever it does.

Then one goes still further. That is, by observing the outward things, one has come to the inner. And the outer and the inner are not two different states; they are the same state of observation out of silence.

This silence is space. We live in a very small space, in the space created by the mind with its own ideas. And the mind is the result of its own conditioning in a particular society and culture; it lives in a very small space; and all the battles, all the relationships, all the anxieties are within that little space. But the moment the mind, through observation, becomes naturally, easily, without effort, silent, that little space is broken. The moment the mind is completely quiet, you will see that there is no limitation to space. You will then see that the object does not create the space, there is space—endless space.

And when that takes place, the mind is the truly religious mind; and from that mind there is activity. You can be a super-citizen—not running away to a monastery, not becoming a sannyasi, or a complete technician, or a mechanized human being. But from that effortless, silent observation, there is action; and that is the only action that does not breed hatred, enmity, competition. Then through observation and silence you will see that, because there is space, there is love.

Love is: dying every day. Love is not memory, love is not thought. Love is not a thing that continues as duration in time. And, through observation, one must die to the continuity of everything. Then there is love; and with love, there comes creation.

Creation is one of the most difficult things to understand. The man who writes a poem, however beautiful, thinks he is a creative being. The man and the woman who breed children think that they are creative. The man or the cook who makes bread thinks, perhaps, he is also creative. But creation is something far more. That man is not creative who merely writes a book or fulfills himself in some petty little ambition. Creation is not a man-made structure, or man-made technological knowledge and the result of technological knowledge, which is merely invention. Creation is something that is timeless, that has no tomorrow and yesterday; it is living timelessly. And you come to it very naturally, if you understand this whole problem of existence.

So a religious mind is all these things, and then it knows, or rather it is in, a state which is creative from moment to moment. It is always acting from that extraordinary sense of emptiness.

I do not know if you have ever noticed how a drum is always empty. When you strike on it, it gives the right tone; but it is empty. Our minds are never empty—they are always full. Therefore, our action is always from this dreadful noise of thought, of memory, of despair; and, therefore, action is always contradictory, leading to great misery.

But a mind that is completely empty—empty in the sense of observation, silence, and therefore, love and the whole understanding of death—such a mind is creative. And a creative mind is empty all the time; it acts from that emptiness, it speaks from that emptiness. And therefore, it will always be true, it will never bring about a deception within itself. And it is only such a religious mind that can solve the problems of misery in this world.

Madras, 7th Public Talk, January 6, 1965
Collected Works, Vol. XV, pp. 46-8

A man who would find a new life, a new way of living, must inquire, must capture this extraordinary quality of silence.

So silence, meditation, and death are very closely related. If there is no death to yesterday, silence is not possible. And silence is necessary, absolutely necessary, for an action which is not accumulative, and in which, therefore, there is no inertia being built up. Death becomes an ugly, frightful thing when you are going to lose what you have accumulated. But if there is no accumulation at all, all through life, from now on, then there is no—what you call—death; living then is dying, and the two are not separate.

The living which we know is a misery, confusion, turmoil, torture, effort, with an occasional, fleeting glance at beauty and love and joy. And that is the result of this consciousness which is inert, which is in itself incapable of new action. A man who would find a new life, a new way of living, must inquire, must capture this extraordinary quality of silence. And there can be silence only when there is death to the past, without argument, without motive, without saying, "I will get a reward." This whole process is meditation. That gives you an extraordinary alertness of mind. There is not a spot in it where there is darkness. There are no unexamined recesses which nothing has touched—meaning that there are no recesses which you have not examined.

So meditation is an extraordinary thing; it is a tremendous joy in itself. For then, in that is silence which in itself is action; silence is inherent in itself, which is action. Then life, everyday living, can be lived out of silence, not out of knowledge—except technological knowledge. And that is the only mutation that man can ever hope to come by. Otherwise, we lead an existence that has no meaning except sorrow and misery and confusion.

Madras, 5th Public Talk, January 5, 1966
Collected Works, Vol. XVI, pp. 31-2

Inquiry means a mind that is sane, healthy, that is not persuaded by opinions of its own or of another, so that it is able to see very clearly, every minute, everything as it moves, as it flows. Life is a movement in relationship, which is action. And unless there is freedom, mere revolt has no meaning at all. A really religious man is never in revolt. He is a free man—free, not from nationalism, greed, envy and all the rest of it; he is just free.

Madras, 1st Public Talk, December 16, 1964
Collected Works, Vol. XV, p. 5

It is learning that will break up the dead things; it is learning that will give the feeling to action. You may make a mistake in that action, but that mistake is a constant process of learning.

I feel that a mind which is not capable of seeing and feeling totally the beauty of the earth, the sky, the palm tree, the horizon, the beauty of a line, a face, a gesture, will never comprehend that extraordinary thing which is beauty and freedom. For most of us freedom is merely the opposite of bondage, therefore merely a reaction. But to comprehend the feeling, the beauty, the loveliness, that extraordinary state which is not the opposite of bondage, requires a mind that is capable of seeing the totality of something. Most of us, surely, have lost or have never had real feeling. Our education, our way of life, our daily habits, traditions, customs have deprived the mind of feeling. If you observe, go into your own mind very diligently, you will find that feeling itself has no motive—the feeling for a tree, the sense of appreciation of a rich man driving a beautiful car, the sight of the villager starving, struggling, toiling day after day. If there is feeling, then from that feeling itself there is an action which is much more comprehensive, much more potent than the intellectual action of the do-gooders and the reformers, because in it there is understanding, a feeling for both the ugly and the beautiful—but not as opposites. To have such feeling is essential if we are to understand this whole process of our existence and our ways of thinking. It means comprehending the depth, the width of life, and also this extraordinary thing called the self, the 'me'. To understand this 'me', this self, with all its joys, its struggles, its pains, intentions, hopes, fears, ambition, envy, jealousy and so on, there must be deep feeling, not mere intellection. You know, when you have a feeling for something, you see much more sharply, much more intelligently and clearly. I do not know if you have noticed it, but when you love somebody, or when you see something rather extraordinary about someone, you become much more intelligent, sharp, alert, do you not? There is a sharpness, an alertness from concentration, but in that there is no feeling, no affection.

If one can really grasp this, not merely intellectually or verbally but actually, seriously, then when you see something—a tree, a boy, a girl—with this quality you can also be aware of the whole content of the mind, not merely the superficial, the obvious, conscious mind but the unconscious with all the innumerable struggles, the racial inheritance, the motives and experiences and stored-up knowledge. From that fullness of awareness and feeling, you will see a totally different process of action taking place.

Perhaps I am talking about something of which you have had no experience, and probably you will tell me to be practical and come down to earth and tell you what to do and not to do, and not be vague. But you see, the difficulty is that unless you see this—unless you see the whole sky, the beauty of the night, of the morning and the evening— you can never do anything worthwhile under the heavens, except your petty little activities of daily existence. Unless you grasp this whole thing, your existence will remain miserable, sorrowful; but with the perception of this enormous thing called life, with the feeling for it, you can come to the practical with precision, with clarity, with depth. But most of us are merely concerned with immediate profit, with immediate results, the immediate pleasure or pain. So it seems to me it is very important, in the pursuit of the understanding of the self, that there be this feeling. But most of our feelings are dead, because when you see every day the same poverty, the same squalor, the same misery and struggle, and the same customs and habits, the mind gets dull, deadened, insensitive, and it becomes very difficult to feel. So, if I may, I would like to go into something which, if we can understand it very deeply, will help us to realize this feeling—the feeling which is quite different from sentimentality, from emotion, tears, and devotion. If we can get this feeling then the heavens will open.

* * * * *

If you are listening—which is an act of attention, not concentration—and directly experiencing your own state, then you will see that an extraordinary feeling of the love of learning comes into being, which is not the learning from a book, from a talk. That kind of learning is merely knowledge; it is dead, it has no meaning; it is only the cultivation of memory, and memory is not intelligence. If you and I can really listen, learn, you will see the turmoil of feeling arising; I am using that word *turmoil* in the right sense—a bubbling, a release of fullness without which there can be no understanding.

* * * * *

If we follow this carefully, we are going to find out how, through attachment, we are destroying feeling, because all our attachment is to

93

dead things. You can never be attached to a living thing any more than you can be attached to the river, to the sea, because the living thing is moving, eternal, in a state of continual motion. So when you say you are attached to your son, your daughter, your husband, if you can very carefully look within yourself, you will see that you cannot be attached to a living person because that person is constantly changing, moving, in a state of turmoil. What you are attached to is your picture of that person... But the picture is a dead thing! So look what the mind is doing—it is creating pictures and attaching itself to dead things!

* * * * *

So you begin to see that love knows no attachment. That is a hard thing to swallow, but it is a fact. And because our minds are so attached to dead things, problems arise. Then we try to cultivate detachment—which is attachment in a different cloak and therefore still in the field of death. Do observe in yourself how dead we are, how we have destroyed the bubbling feeling. The earth is not a dead thing, but when you are attached to something you call "India," which is just a symbol of a small part and not the earth itself, then you are clinging to something which is dead. Therefore your nationalism is merely a flirtation with death; it has no depth, no vitality. But the feeling for the earth itself—not my earth or the Russian, American or English earth—that has a living quality.

* * * * *

Now, if you have really understood all this, not merely verbally or intellectually, but if you feel deeply with me that this is really a very serious thing, then you will see that you can go to the office, take a bus, function in everyday life with a different quality, a new quality of mind. After all, you cannot stop doing your regular jobs, living your daily life; now it is a routine to which you are attached. And when you are attached to the fountain that holds the water you cannot move with the living water. To see the truth of this requires not only insight, clarity of thought, precision of mind, but also the sense of beauty. If you have understood, you will see that attachment has no meaning any more. You do not have to struggle to be free of it; it drops away like a leaf in the wind. Then your mind becomes extraordinarily alive, sharp, precise, no longer confused.

* * * * *

I hope I have made myself clear, because for most of us the day-to-day action of habit has become all-important, so that we never see the horizon but are always doing something. You can only have the explosion of feeling when you understand this whole process of yourself and your attachments. If you can explore, examine, look into this thing called attachment, then you will begin to learn, and it is learning that will break up the dead things; it is learning that will give the feeling to action. You may make a mistake in that action, but that mistake is a constant process of learning. To act means that you are trying to see, to find out, to understand, not merely trying to produce a result—which is a dead result. Action becomes very small and petty if you do not understand the center, the actor. We separate the actor from the action; the 'I' always does that and so becomes a dead thing. But if you are beginning to understand yourself, which is self-knowledge, which is learning about yourself, then that learning is a beautiful thing, so subtle, like living waters. If you understand that, and with that understanding act—not with the action of thought, but through the very process of learning—then you will find that the mind is no longer dead, no longer attached to dead and dying things. The mind, then, is extraordinary; it is like the horizon, endless, like space, without measure. Such a mind can go very deeply and become that which is the universe, the timeless. From that state you will be able to act in time, but with a totally different feeling. All this requires not chronological time, days, weeks, and years, but the understanding of yourself, which can be done immediately. You will know, then, what love is. Love knows no jealousy, no envy, no ambition, and has no anchorage; it is a state in which there is no time, and because of that, action takes on a totally different meaning in our daily existence.

Bombay, 4th Public Talk, December 7, 1958
Collected Works, Vol. XI, pp. 120-3

VI.
Krishnamurti: His Heuristic Approach

That truth acts which has been discovered by you.

When you discover for yourself what is true, then that truth acts. You do not have to act at all. Even in your office, in your home, when you are walking by yourself in solitude among woods and streams, that truth acts which has been discovered by you—not repeated by you because you have heard it said by somebody else. When you discover for yourself what is true and what is false, when you discover for yourself the truth in the false and the truth as truth, then that extraordinary thing has a quality of explosion; and that explosive quality heals and brings about action out of that pure health and clarity. That is what we are going to do this evening. By listening to the words of the speaker, you are going to discover for yourself the truth, and then let the truth operate, where it will, when it will. And when it operates, let it operate without your interference.

Bombay, 4th Public Talk, February 19, 1964
Collected Works, Vol. XIV, pp. 143-4

It is self-knowledge that brings clarity, not dependence on a book, a teacher, or a guide.

Please, as I am talking, look at your own life; observe your own daily activities, observe your thoughts. I am only describing what is actually taking place. If you merely listen to the words and do not relate what is being said to the activities of your own mind, it will have no meaning at all. But if you can relate what is being said to your everyday life, to the actual state of your own mind, then the talk will have an immense significance, because then you will find that I am not telling you what to do; on the contrary, through the description, through the explanation, you are going to discover for yourself the process of your own thinking. And when you understand yourself, clarity comes. It is self-knowledge that brings clarity, not dependence on a book, a teacher, or a guide. To observe how you think, the manner of your response to challenge in your various relationships—to be aware of all that, not theoretically but actually, will reveal the process of yourself; and in that understanding there is clarity. So please, if I may most earnestly request it, listen and relate what you hear to the actual state of your own mind. Then these talks will be worthwhile; otherwise they will be mere words to be soon forgotten.

Colombo, Sri Lanka, 2nd Public Talk, January 16, 1957
Collected Works, Vol. X, pp. 204-5

Have you ever looked at a flower without calling it a rose...?

Now, is it possible to see, to observe, to be aware of the beautiful and the ugly things of life, and not say, "I must have" or "I must not have"? Have you ever just observed anything? Do you understand, sirs? Have you ever observed your wife, your children, your friends, just looked at them? Have you ever looked at a flower without calling it a rose, without wanting to put it in your buttonhole, or take it home and give it to somebody? If you are capable of so observing, without all the values attributed by the mind, then you will find that desire is not such a monstrous thing. You can look at a car, see the beauty of it, and not be caught in the turmoil or contradiction of desire. But that requires an immense intensity of observation, not just a casual glance. It is not that you have no desire, but simply that the mind is capable of looking without describing. It can look at the moon and not immediately say, "That is the moon, how beautiful it is," so there is no chattering of the mind coming in between. If you can do this, you will find that in the intensity of observation, of feeling, of real affection, love has its own action, which is not the contradictory action of desire.

Bombay, 2nd Public Talk, February 10, 1957
Collected Works, Vol. X, p. 245

"But I _do_ want to change."

Now, what is it that makes you move, act?

"Any strong feeling. Intense anger makes me act; I may afterwards regret it, but the feeling explodes into action."

That is, your whole being is in it; you forget or disregard danger, you are lost to your own safety, security. The very feeling is action; there is no gap between the feeling and the act. The gap is created by the so-called reasoning process, a weighing of the pros and the cons according to one's convictions, prejudices, fears, and so on. Action is then political, it is stripped of spontaneity, of all humanity. The men who are seeking power, whether for themselves, their group or their country, act in this manner, and such action only breeds further misery and confusion.

"Actually," went on the man from the office, "even a strong feeling for fundamental change is soon erased by self-protective reasoning, by thinking what would happen if such a change took place in one, and so on."

The feeling is then hedged about by ideas, by words, is it not? There is a contradictory reaction, born of the desire not to be disturbed. If that is the case, then continue in your old way; don't deceive yourself by following the ideal, by saying that you are trying to change, and all the rest of it. Be simple with the fact that you don't want to change. The realization of this truth is in itself sufficient.

"But I _do_ want to change."

Then change; but don't talk unfeelingly about the necessity of changing. It has no meaning.

"At my age," said the old man, "I have nothing to lose in the outward sense; but to give up the old ideas and conclusions is quite another matter. I now see at least one thing: that there can be no fundamental change without an awakening of the feeling for it. Reasoning is necessary, but it's not the instrument of action. To know is not necessarily to act."

But the action of feeling is also the action of knowing, the two are not separate; they are separate only when reason, knowledge, conclusion or belief induces action.

"I am beginning to see this very clearly, and my knowledge of the Scriptures, as a basis for action, is already losing its grip on my mind."

Action based on authority is no action at all; it is mere imitation, repetition.

"And most of us are caught in that process. But one can break away from it. I have understood a great deal this evening."

Commentaries On Living Series III, pp. 161-2

It is only in the immediate that there can be order...

If I postpone action, if I say I will change tomorrow, between now and tomorrow every kind of pressure, influence, every kind of movement is taking place. Therefore time does not produce order. It is only in the immediate that there can be order, not through time. There can be order only when one understands the whole structure and nature of time.

Paris, 4th Public Talk, May 27, 1965
Collected Works, Vol. XV, p. 175

The explanation is simple; but to see it, to break it down...that means instant action.

The very resistance to life is conflict. So we have to enquire what life is. All that I know is to resist life, life being this extraordinary movement. I don't know what that movement is; it's a movement, an endless current. And all that I've learned [as] a human being, for ten thousand years, is to build walls around myself. The very building of those walls is a resistance, and therefore conflict. The explanation is simple; but to see it, to break it down, to see the resistance, to be aware of the heavily guarded resistance, strengthened through centuries—that means instant action.

Rome, 2nd Public Discussion, April 3, 1966
Collected Works, Vol. XVI, p. 99

To explore, to discover, there must be joy, there must be enthusiasm, vitality, especially when going into this complex thing called the mind.

I would like to talk about action which is not partial, which is not the outcome of knowledge, which is not the product of authority, but something entirely different—which means, really, action without a center. It must have happened to you that you have done something without calculation, without argumentation, without the cunning machinations of thought, without thinking of what has been or what may be, without choice. You must have done something in your life without this whole process taking place. But to understand this kind of action requires a great deal of self-knowledge, which is comprehension of the workings of one's own mind; because it is so easy to deceive oneself and say, "I have acted without a center, I have joined such and such a group without the process of thought"—which is idiotic and immature, for what is functioning is one's own hidden desire. Whereas, action which is total, and which has no center, requires exploration into oneself—and this means, really, going into the whole process of thinking, into the whole mechanism of the mind, without a limit, without an end in view.

I do not know if any of you have ever seriously gone into yourselves with complete willingness, with wholeheartedness, with joy, without any sense of compulsion, and have tried to discover what you are. Merely to say, "I am this" or "I am not that," is again immature, it has no meaning. To explore, to discover, there must be joy, there must be enthusiasm, vitality, especially when going into this complex thing called the mind. But most of us explore either out of despair, or to find something which will give us nourishment, which will give us stability, an assurance of continuity. Real inquiry must be without any of these things. One inquires just to find out what is actually taking place. I do not know if you have ever done that, if you have ever studied yourself as a woman studies her face in a mirror. There is nothing wrong with studying your face in a mirror, which is to see it exactly as it is—straight hair, crooked nose, and so on. You can embellish it, color it, try to make it more beautiful, but that is another matter. Similarly, to study yourself is to see what is actually the state of your mind— why you think and do certain things, why you go to the office or to the temple, why you talk in a certain way to your wife, to your servant, why you read the sacred books, why you attend these talks. You have

101

to know all this from moment to moment, not as accumulated knowledge on the basis of which you function. Learning is a movement of the mind in which there is no accumulation. You can learn only when knowledge is not being gathered from the movement of learning. The moment you gather knowledge, add to what you have learned, you have ceased to learn. A mind that gathers knowledge through learning is driven by the desire for safety, security, or is out for some profit. Whereas, in the movement of learning there is no accumulation—and that is the beauty of learning. To learn is just to see what you are—the hate, the calumny, the vulgarity, the fears, the hopes, the anxieties, the ambitions—without judging, without evaluating, without condemning or accepting.

Madras, 3rd Public Talk, November 29, 1959
Collected Works, Vol. XI, pp. 226-7

If you observe this whole process of yourself in the mirror of relationship, that is the one necessary action.

The questioner asks, "Is not a certain amount of disciplinary training necessary to understand what you are teaching?" If you love to do something, is it necessary to discipline yourself to do it? If you are really interested in what I am saying, do you need discipline? Must you train your mind to pay complete attention, to listen with deep feeling? That very listening is the act of understanding—but you are not interested. That is the real problem: you are not interested. Not that you should be. But fundamentally you are superficial; you want an easy way of existence, you want to get on. It is too much of a bother to think very deeply, and besides, you might have to act deeply, you might find yourself in total revolt against this rotten society. So you play with it, you keep one foot here and one foot there, tottering and asking, "Should I discipline myself in order to understand?" Whereas, if you really inquired into what I am teaching, you would find it very simple; and you can do it yourself, you need no assistance from anybody, including myself. All that you have to do is to understand the operation of your own mind—and a marvelous thing it is, the mind; the most beautiful thing on earth.

But we are not interested in that. We are interested in what the mind can get for us in the way of security, passion, power, position, knowledge—which are the various centers of self-interest. And I say, look at the operation of your own mind, go into it, understand it, all of which you can do by yourself; watch your everyday relationship with people, the way you talk, the way you gesticulate, your pursuit of power, how you behave in front of the important man and in front of the servant. If you observe this whole process of yourself in the mirror of relationship, that is the one necessary action. You don't have to do anything about it, but merely observe it. If you observe, go into the whole process of yourself without condemnation, you will find that the mind becomes extraordinarily sharp, clear, and fearless; therefore, the mind is capable of understanding such human problems as death, meditation, dreams, and the many other things that confront it.

So you don't need any special training. What you need is to pay attention, not to what I say, but to your own mind; you must see for yourself how it is caught in words, in explanations without any basis, without any reality. Perhaps it is the reality of someone else, but if you make that the basis of your life, then it is not reality, it is merely a supposition, a speculation, an imagination, and therefore it is without validity, it has no reality behind it. To find reality you have to work as hard as you work for your daily living, and much harder, because all this is much more subtle, requiring greater attention; for every movement of thought indicates a state of the mind, of the conscious as well as the unconscious. As you cannot observe the operation of your mind all the time, you pick it up, observe it, and let it go. If you watch yourself in this manner you will find that attention has quite a different significance, and that you can free the mind from the collective. As long as the mind is merely a record of the collective, it is of no more value than a machine. The new computers are extraordinarily capable along certain lines, but human beings are something more than that. They have the possibility of that extraordinary creativity which is not just the writing of poems or books, but the creativity of a mind that has no center.

Madras, 3rd Public Talk, December 19, 1956
Collected Works, Vol. X, pp. 180-1

I wonder if you have ever walked along a crowded street, or a lonely road, and just looked at things without thought?

Is it possible to live in this world and go to the office, cook, wash dishes, drive a car, and do all the other daily things of life which at present have become repetitive and breed conflict—is it possible to do all these things, to live and to act, without any ideation, and thereby free action from all contradiction?

I wonder if you have ever walked along a crowded street, or a lonely road, and just looked at things without thought? There is a state of observation without the interference of thought. Though you are aware of everything about you, and you may recognize the person, the mountain, the tree, or the oncoming car, yet the mind is not functioning in the usual pattern of thought. I don't know if this has ever happened to you. Do try it sometime when you are driving or walking. Just look without thought; observe without the reaction which breeds thought. Though you recognize color and form, though you see the stream, the car, the goat, the bus, there is no reaction, but merely negative observation; and that very state of so-called negative observation is action. Such a mind can utilize knowledge in carrying out what it has to do, but it is free of thought in the sense that it is not functioning in terms of reaction. With such a mind—a mind that is attentive without reaction—you can go to the office and all the rest of it.

Most of us are everlastingly thinking about ourselves from morning till night, and we function within the pattern of that self-centered activity. All such activity, which is a reaction, is bound to lead to various forms of conflict and deterioration. And is it possible not to function within that pattern, and yet to live in this world? I don't mean living off by yourself in some mountain cave, and all that kind of thing; but is it possible to live in this world and to function as a total human being from a state of emptiness—if you will not misunderstand my use of that word? Whether you paint, or write poems, or go to an office, or talk, can you always have inwardly an empty space, and through that empty space, work? For when there is this empty space, action does not breed contradiction.

I think this is a very important thing to discover—and you have to discover it for yourself, because it cannot be taught or explained. To discover it, you must first understand how all self-centered action breeds conflict, and then ask yourself whether the mind can ever be content with such action. It may be momentarily satisfied; but when you perceive that in all such action conflict is inevitable, you are already trying to find out if there is another kind of action, an action which does not lead to conflict; and then you are bound to come upon the fact that there is.

Saanen, 7th Public Talk, July 26, 1964
Collected Works, Vol. XIV, pp. 205-6

When you meet the fact...then you are living completely in the present.

So a mind is free only when it is capable of meeting the fact, the *what is*, meeting poverty [for example], not some supreme challenge— there is no supreme challenge. Life is a challenge every minute: meeting poverty; meeting your boss in your office; meeting your wife, the children; meeting the bus conductor, the squalor, the beauty of a sunset; your own anger, jealousy, stupidity—which are all facts. What matters is how you meet the fact, not what you think about it, not what you should do about it. When you meet the fact, without any opinion, judgment, evaluation, then you are living completely in the present. Then for such a mind there is no time, and therefore it can act. Because the fact alone has the urgency of action—not your opinions, desires, and ideals.

Madras, 4th Public Talk, December 27, 1964
Collected Works, Vol. XV, p. 25

To be sensitive implies a state of mind in which there is only the fact, and not all your memories about that fact. Such perception, such seeing, such listening at every moment has an extraordinary action in life. Please don't be carried away by the speaker's intensity or enthusiasm. Don't get mesmerized, but watch, listen, and find out for yourself.

Saanen, 3rd Public Talk, July 26, 1962
Collected Works, Vol. XIII, p. 229

...when you are capable of looking purely at a fact of any kind—the fact of memory, the fact of jealousy, the fact of nationalism, the fact of hatred, the desire for power, position, prestige—then the fact reveals an immense power. Then the fact flowers and in the flowering of the fact is not only the understanding of the fact, but the action which is produced by the fact.

...It is only out of the pure act of seeing the fact [that] there comes the action, the mutation in human consciousness.

Madras, 2nd Public Talk, November 26,1961
Collected Works, Vol. XII, p. 283

This fact has to be seen: that there is a dimension of action which does not breed conflict or sorrow. And to find it, to come upon it darkly, mysteriously, without thinking, there must be freedom right from the beginning, not at the end—freedom to investigate, to look, to observe; freedom from fear.

Bombay, 3rd Public Talk, February 20, 1966
Collected Works, Vol. XVI, p. 59

The problem, if you love it, is as beautiful as the sunset. If you are antagonistic to the problem, you will never understand.

Most of you put questions and expect an answer, "yes" or "no." It is easy to ask questions like "What do you mean?" and then sit back and let me explain, but it is much more arduous to find out the answer for yourselves, go into the problem so profoundly, so clearly and without any corruption that the problem ceases to be. That can only happen when the mind is really silent in the face of the problem. The problem, if you love it, is as beautiful as the sunset. If you are antagonistic to the problem, you will never understand. Most of us are antagonistic because we are frightened of the result, of what may happen if we proceed, so we lose the significance and the purview of the problem.

The First and Last Freedom, pp. 244-5

One sees very clearly that only when the image doesn't interfere—image as knowledge, thought, emotion, all the rest of it—only then can I look, can I hear, can I understand. It has happened to all of us. When suddenly, after you discuss, argue, point out, and so on, suddenly your mind becomes quiet and you see that, and you say, "By Jove, I've understood." That understanding is an action, not an idea. Right?

Ojai, 5th Public Talk, November 12, 1966
Collected Works, Vol. XVII, p. 82

Because you understand, that very understanding is an action which goes on and on in spite of you, whether you like it or not.

So the conscious mind, by observing the necessity of quietness, is quiet. Then the unconscious projects all the things, all its contents; as you observe a tree, as you observe a woman, as you observe a man, as you observe a child, as all the responses, the motives, the hidden dark corners of the mind spill out; and they are understood immediately because the conscious mind is not judging, is not evaluating, is not comparing. It is there, watching, completely still, because it is no longer seeking, no longer wanting experience. Then you will see, if you have gone as far as that, that the whole content of consciousness is empty.

These are not words. Don't repeat it afterwards and ask, "How is the conscious to be emptied?" Either you are doing it or you will never do it. If you are doing it, you will go on for the rest of your life. If you are not doing it now, you will never do it; because this is not an act of memory, this is an act in the living present. Because you understand, that very understanding is an action which goes on and on in spite of you, whether you like it or not.

New Delhi, 6th Public Talk, November 10, 1963
Collected Works, Vol. XIV, pp. 38-9

I hope all this is not too abstract and too difficult; but even if it is, please listen. Although you may not fully understand what is being said, the very act of listening is like planting a seed in the dark soil. If the seed is vital, and if the soil is rich, it will produce a shoot; you don't have to do a thing about it. Similarly, if you can just listen and let the seed fall in the womb of the mind, it will germinate, it will flourish and bring about an action which is unconsciously true.

New Delhi, 8th Public Talk, March 4, 1959
Collected Works, Vol. XI, p. 199

VII.
"The Individual's Responsibility is Not to Society, But to Himself."

The individual is obviously of the greatest significance in society, because it is only the individual who is capable of creative activity, not the mass.

This evening I would like to suggest that we talk over the question of change and revolution; but before we go into it, I think it is very important to understand the relationship of the individual to society. The first thing to realize is that the problems of the individual, his sorrows and struggles, are also those of the world. The world is the individual; the individual is not different from the society in which he lives. That is why, without a radical transformation of the individual, society becomes a burden, an irresponsible continuity in which the individual is merely a cog.

There is a strong tendency to think that the individual is of little importance in modern society, and that everything possible must be done to control the individual, to shape his thought through propaganda, through sanctions, through the various means of mass communication. The individual himself wonders what he can do in a society which is so burdensome, which bears down on him with the weight of a mountain, and he feels almost helpless. Confronted with this mass of confusion, deterioration, war, starvation, and misery, the individual not unnaturally puts to himself the question, "What can I do?" And I think the answer to this question is that he cannot do anything, which is an obvious fact. He can't prevent a war, he can't do away with starvation, he can't put a stop to religious bigotry, or to the historical process of nationalism, with all its conflicts.

So I think to put such a question is inherently wrong. The individual's responsibility is not to society, but to himself. And if he is responsible to himself, he will act upon society—but not the other way round. Obviously the individual can't do anything about this social confusion; but when he begins to clear up his own confusion, his self-contradiction, his own violence and fears, then such an individual has an extraordinary importance in society. I think very few of us realize this. Seeing that we cannot do anything on a world scale, we invariably do nothing at all, which is really an escape from the action within oneself which will bring about a radical change.

So I am talking to you as one individual to another. We are not communicating with each other as Indians, or Americans, or Russians, or Chinese, nor as members of any particular group. We are talking things over as two human beings, not as a layman and a specialist. If that much is clear between us, we can proceed.

The individual is obviously of the greatest significance in society, because it is only the individual who is capable of creative activity, not the mass—and I shall explain presently what I mean by that word *creative*. If you see this fact, then you will also realize that what you are in yourself is of the highest importance. Your capacity to think, to function with wholeness, with an integration in which there is no self-contradiction—this has an enormous significance.

We see that if there is to be any real change in the world—and there must be a real change—then you and I as individuals will have to transform ourselves. Unless there is a radical change in each one of us, life becomes an endless imitation, ultimately leading to boredom, frustration, and hopelessness.

Now, what do we mean by change? Surely, change under compulsion is no change at all. If I change because society forces me to change, it is merely an adjustment according to convenience, a conformity brought about by pressure, by fear.

Most of us change only under compulsion, through fear, through some form of reward or punishment. Psychologically, this is the actual fact. And when we are forced to change, it is merely an outward conformity, while inwardly we remain the same. I may change because my family or the society in which I live influences me to do so, or because the government requires that I act in a certain way; but this is only an adjustment, it is not change, and inwardly I am still greedy, envious, ambitious, frustrated, sorrowful, fearful. I have outwardly conformed to a new pattern; I have not changed radically within myself. And is it possible for me as a human being to be in a state of continuous change, revolution, which is not the result of any compulsion or promise of reward?

Surely, anything I do because of compulsion, fear, imitation, or reward, is within the field of time, and it breeds habit. I do the thing over and over again until habit is established, and this habit is within the field of time. So there can be no real change, no revolution, within the field of time; there can only be adjustment, conformity, imitation, habit. Change requires a total perception or awareness of all that is implied in imitation, conformity, and this total perception frees the mind to change radically. I am just introducing it to you, so that you and I can think it out together.

As I said, any form of change through compulsion is no change at all, which I think is fairly obvious. If you force your child to do something, he will do it through fear, but there is no understanding, no comprehension of what is involved. When action is born of fear, outwardly it may appear to be a change, but actually it is not.

Now, let us find out if it is possible to understand and free the mind from fear, so that there is a change without effort. All effort to change implies an inducement, does it not? When I make an effort to change, it is in order to gain, to avoid, or to become something; therefore there is no radical change at all. I think this fact must be very clearly understood by each one of us if there is to be a fundamental change.

If we are well off and have a good job, if we are fairly well-to-do, most of us are contented and do not want anything changed; we just want to carry on as we are. We have fallen into a certain habit, a certain comfortable groove, and we want to continue in that state of endless limitation. But the wave of life does not function in that way; it is always beating upon and breaking down the walls of security which we have built around ourselves. Our desire to be secure right through, psychologically as well as physically, is constantly being challenged by the movement of life, which like a restless sea is always pounding on the shore. And nothing can withstand that pounding; however much one may cling to inward security, life will not allow it to exist for long. So there is a contradiction between the movement of life and our desire to be secure; and out of this comes fear in all its various forms.

If we can understand fear, perhaps in the very process of that understanding there will be the cessation of fear, and therefore a fundamental change without effort.

111

What is fear? I do not know if you have ever thought about it. We are going to examine it now; but if you merely follow verbally what is said and are not aware of your own fear, then you will not understand and will not be free of fear.

After all, these meetings are intended not merely to stimulate you but to help to bring about a change in the quality of the mind. That is where there must be a revolution: in the quality of the mind itself. And that revolution can take place only if you are aware of your own fear, and are capable of looking at it directly.

Fear is a sorrowful, a dreadful thing, and it is always following most of us like a shadow. One may not be aware of it, but deep down it is there: the fear of death, the fear of failure, the fear of losing a job, the fear of what the neighbors will say, the fear of one's wife or husband, and so on. There are fears of which one is conscious, and fears of which one is unaware. I am not talking about a particular form of fear, but of the whole sense of fear; because unless the mind is free from all sense of fear—which is not to cover it up—thought cannot function with clarity, with perception; there is always apprehension, confusion. So it is absolutely essential for the individual to be free from fear in all its forms.

Now, how does fear arise? Is there fear when you are actually confronted with the fact? Please follow this closely. Is there fear when you are face to face with the fact of death, let us say? Surely, when you are directly confronted with the fact, there is no fear, because in that moment the challenge demands your action and you respond, you act. Fear arises only before or after the event. I am afraid of death in the future. I am afraid of what may happen if I become ill—I may lose my job. Or I am afraid at the thought of what has already happened, or what nearly happened. So my fear is always linked to the past or to the future, it is always within the brackets of time, is it not? Fear is the result of my thinking about the past, and of my thinking about the future. If you observe very carefully you will see that there is no fear of the present. That is because when there is full awareness of the present, neither the past nor the future exists. I do not know if I am making myself clear on this point.

Knowing that I shall die in the future, I am afraid of death, of what is going to be. I have seen death in the past, and that has awakened in me fear of what is going to happen in the future. So my mind is never fully aware of the present—which does not mean that I must live thoughtlessly in the present. I am talking about an awareness of

112

the present which is not contaminated by past fear or future fear, and which is therefore limitless.

This is very difficult to understand unless you experience for yourself what I am talking about—or rather, unless you observe the actual arising of fear. Fear comes into being only when thought is caught in the past as memory, or in the future as anticipation. So time is the factor of fear, and until the mind is free of time there can be no radical wiping away of fear. It sounds complicated, but it is not. We are used to resisting fear, to disciplining ourselves against it. We say that we must not think about the past or the future, that we must live only in the present; therefore we build a wall of resistance against the past and the future and try to make the best of the present, which is a very shallow way of living. If that is clear, let us look again at the whole process of fear.

Being afraid, how am I to resolve fear? I may resist fear, I may escape from it; but resistance and escape do not wipe away fear. How then am I to approach fear, how am I to understand and resolve it without effort? The moment I make an effort to be free of fear, I am exercising will, which is a form of resistance; and resistance does not bring understanding. So this habit of effort must go—that is the first thing I have to realize. My mind is caught in the habit of condemning, resisting fear, which prevents the understanding of fear. If I want to understand fear, there must be no resistance, no defense mechanism in operation with regard to that particular feeling which I call fear. And then what happens? What happens when the mind is free from the habit of resisting or running away from fear through reading books, listening to the radio, and through the various other forms of escape with which we are all familiar? Then, surely, the mind is capable of looking directly at that feeling which it calls fear.

Now, can the mind look at anything without naming it? Can I look at a flower, at the moonlight on the water, at an insect, at a feeling, without verbalizing it, without giving it a name? Because verbalizing, giving a name to what is perceived, is a distraction from perceiving, is it not?

Please, sirs, I hope you are actually doing this, experimenting to find out whether you can look at your fear without naming it. Can you look at a flower without giving it a name, without saying, "It is lovely", "It is yellow", "I like that flower", "I don't like that flower"—without all the chattering of the mind that comes into operation when you look at something? Try it and you will find that it is one of the most difficult things to do. This chattering of the mind, this verbalization in terms of condemnation or admiration, is a habit that prevents direct perception.

So you are now aware of your fear; you know you are afraid. Can you look at it without condemnation or acceptance? Are you looking at it through the focus of the word *fear*, or are you aware of that feeling without the word?

Sirs, let us take another example. Most of us are idolatrous—which means that the symbol becomes extraordinarily significant. We worship not only the idol made by the hand, but also the ideal created by thought. Now, an idolatrous mind is not a free mind. An idolatrous mind can never think clearly, perceptively. The man who has an ideal is obviously not very thoughtful. I know it is the fashion to have ideals; it is the respectable escape from the actual fact, and that is why ideals become all-important. But however much you may pursue the ideal of non- violence, for example, the actual fact is that you are violent.

So the idealistic mind is idolatrous; being violent, it worships the ideal of non-violence, and thereby lives in a state of self-contradiction. The ideal of non-violence is merely the mind's reaction against its own violence; and if it is to be free of both, the mind must be aware of the fact of its violence, but not in relation to the opposite, which it calls non-violence. Then one can look at violence, observe it with one's whole being, which is not to condemn it, or say that it is inevitable in life.

Now, are you aware of your fear in that way? Are you aware of the feeling without the word? That is, can you look at the feeling without verbalizing it—which is really to give your whole attention to the feeling, is it not? There is then no distraction, no verbal screen between you and what is being observed. That is true perception, surely: when the mind is not chattering but sees the fact entirely, without the word coming in between.

This observation of fear without verbalization is in itself discipline; it is not a discipline imposed upon the mind. I hope this is clear, because it is very important to understand it. The observation of fear is in itself discipline. You don't have to exercise discipline in order to observe. The exercising of discipline in order to observe prevents observation; it blocks perception. But when you see the falseness of disciplining the mind to observe, that very perception brings its own discipline.

If you want to understand something, if you want to understand fear, you must obviously give your whole attention to it. Do not say: "How am I to give my whole attention without discipline?" That is a wrong question, which will receive a wrong answer. First see the truth that to understand your fear, you must give it your whole attention, and that there can be no attention as long as you run away from fear, or condemn it. This condemnation and escape is a habit which you have fallen into, and habit cannot be wiped away by any discipline. The disciplining of the mind to wipe away habit merely creates another habit. But in observing fear without verbalization, without condemnation or justification, there is a spontaneous discipline from moment to moment—which means that the mind is free from the habit of discipline.

I wonder how many of you are following all this? Perhaps you are too tired at the end of the day to follow it consciously; but if you just listen without a conscious effort to listen, I think you will find that listening is in itself an astonishing thing. If you listen rightly, a miracle takes place. The man who knows how to listen without effort learns much more than the man who makes an effort to listen. When one listens easily, effortlessly, the mind can see what is true and what is false; it can see the truth in the false. So listen to what is being said, even though you may not be able to follow it consciously, through direct experience. After all, the deep, fundamental responses of human beings are anonymous. It is not that I am telling you something, which you then understand, but when the mind is in a state of listening there is an understanding which is neither yours nor mine; and it is this effortless understanding that brings about a fundamental revolution.

To go back, fear exists only within the brackets of time, where there is no real change but merely reaction. Communism, for example, is a reaction from capitalism, just as bravery is a reaction from fear. Where there is freedom, which is the absence of fear, there is a state which cannot be called bravery. It is a state of intelligence. That intelligence can meet problems without fear, and therefore understand them. When a mind that is afraid is confronted with a problem, whatever action it takes only further confuses the problem.

So, freeing the mind is the action of intelligence. There is no definition of intelligence, and if you merely pursue a definition you will not be intelligent. But if you begin step by step to find out precisely what you are afraid of and why, then you are bound to discover that there is a division between the observer and the observed. Please follow this a little bit, sirs, I am only putting it differently.

There is the observer who says, "I am afraid," and who is separate from the feeling which he calls fear. If, for example, I am afraid of what the neighbors might say, there is the feeling of fear, and the 'me' who is the experiencer, the observer of that feeling. As long as there is this division between the observer and the observed, between the 'me' who is afraid and the feeling of being afraid, there can be no ending of fear. The ending of fear comes about only when you begin to analyze and examine very carefully the whole process of fear, and discover for yourself that the observer is not different from the observed. There is fear because the observer in himself is afraid, so it is not a matter of being free from the fear of a particular thing. Freedom from the fear of something is a reaction and is therefore not freedom. When I am free from anger, that freedom is merely a reaction from anger, and therefore it is not freedom. When I am free from violence, that freedom is again only a reaction from violence. There is a freedom which is not freedom from something, and which is the highest form of intelligence; but that freedom can come into being only when one goes very deeply into this whole question of fear.

Now, let us look at another problem, which is this: Why do we have ideals? Is it not a waste of time? Do not ideals prevent the perception of what actually is? I know most of you have ideals: the ideal of nobility, the ideal of chastity, the ideal of non-violence, and many more. Why? Do they really help you to get rid of *what is*? I am avaricious, acquisitive, envious, let us say, and I have the ideal of renunciation. Now, why should I have that ideal at all? We say the ideal is necessary because it will act as a lever, as a means of getting rid of avariciousness. But is that so? Surely, the mind can be free of greed, or whatever it is, only when it applies itself to the problem, and not when it is distracted by an ideal. That is why I say the ideal is utter nonsense. Being violent, the mind pursues the ideal of non-violence, which is a vast mechanism of escape from the actual fact of violence. It is a self-deception. It has no validity at all. What has validity is violence and one's capacity to examine it. To pursue the ideal of non-violence, all the time struggling within oneself not to be violent, is another form of violence.

So what matters is not the ideal, but the fact and your capacity to face the fact. You cannot face the fact of your anger, your violence, as long as you have an ideal, because the ideal is fictitious, fallacious, it has no reality. To understand your violence, you must give your whole attention to it, and you cannot give your whole attention to it if you have an ideal. Idealism is merely one of the habits that we have, and India is drowning in this habit. "He is a noble man, he has ideals and conforms to them"—you know all the nonsense we talk. The simple fact is that we are violent; and it is only when we look at our violence without justification or condemnation that we can go into it. The moment one's mind ceases to justify or condemn violence, it is already free to examine the structure of violence.

Fear expresses itself in different forms. There is not only fear as despair, but also fear as hope, and most of us are caught in the chasm between the two. Being in despair, we run to hope; but if we begin to understand the whole process of fear, then there is neither hope nor despair.

Sirs, I do not know if you have ever tried pursuing virtue to its limit and examining it without acceptance or rejection. Try it sometime, try pursuing and looking at virtue without justifying or condemning it, and you will find that you come to a point in the understanding of virtue which is not merely social convenience or conformity to an idealistic pattern. You will come to a point when the mind is free from the whole idea of virtue and therefore faces a state of nothingness.

Again, sirs, please listen before you agree or disagree; just listen, and let the words sink into your unconscious.

The mind is at present cluttered with ideas, is it not? The mind is the result of experience; the mind is fearful, it knows hope and despair, greed and the ideal of non-greed. Being the result of time, the mind can function only within the field of time; and within that field there is no change. Change there is merely imitation or reaction, and therefore it is not a revolution.

Now, if the mind can push more and more deeply into itself, you will find that it comes to a point when there is complete nothingness, a total void, which is not the void of despair. Hope and despair are both the outcome of fear; and when you have deeply pursued fear and gone beyond it, you will come to this state of nothingness, a sense of complete void which is not related to despair. It is only in this state that there is a revolution, a radical transformation in the quality of the mind itself.

But this state of nothingness is not an ideal to be pursued. It has nothing to do with the inventions of the mind. The mind cannot comprehend it, for it is much too vast. But what the mind can do is to free itself from all its chattering, from all its pettiness, from all its stupidities, its envy, greed, fear. When the mind is silent there is the coming into being of this sense of complete nothingness which is the very essence of humility. It is only then that there is a radical transformation in the quality of the mind, and it is only such a mind that is creative.

New Delhi, 4th Public Talk, February 18, 1959
Collected Works, Vol. XI, pp. 171-7

VIII.
The Relation of Action to Other Areas of Inquiry

True action comes from clarity.

For most of us action becomes a routine, a habit, something that one does, not out of love, or because it has deep significance for oneself, but because one has to do it. One is driven to it by circumstances, by a wrong kind of education, by the lack of that love out of which one does something real. If we can go into this whole question, I think it will be very revealing, for then perhaps we shall begin to understand the true nature of revolution.

Surely, true action comes from clarity. When the mind is very clear, unconfused, not contradictory within itself, then action inevitably follows from that clarity; we need not be concerned with how to bring about action. But it is very difficult, is it not, to have undisturbed perception and to see things, not as one would like to see them, but as they actually are, undistorted by one's likes and dislikes. It is only out of such clarity that the fullness of action takes place.

* * * * *

Clarity is of far greater significance than action. But our minds are ridden by systems, by techniques, by the desire to know what to do. The "what to do?" has become very important, it is our everlasting question. We want to know what to do about starvation, what to do about inequality, about the appalling corruption in the world, and about our own sorrow and suffering. We are always looking for a method, a means, a system of action, are we not?

But how to find clarity is obviously a much more significant inquiry, because if one can think very clearly, if one has perception

119

which is not distorted, which is direct, complete, then from that clear perception, action follows. Such clarity creates its own action. But people who are dedicated to various systems are always at loggerheads with each other, are they not? They cannot work together. Each interprets the problem in terms of the system to which he is committed, according to his particular conditioning and self-interest. I do not know if you have ever noticed how most of us divide ourselves into groups, parties, and systems, and commit ourselves to certain conclusions. Any such commitment, surely, does not bring clarity. It brings only enmity, opposition. But if you and I approach our human problems, not with commitments, conclusions, and self-interest, but with clarity, then I think these problems can very easily be solved.

* * * * *

So the real problem is the mind that approaches the problem; and may I suggest that we not merely listen to what is being said, but go into ourselves and find out in what manner the mind is confused. If we ask how to clear up our confusion, it will only bring about the cultivation of another system. To actually see that the mind is confused has far greater significance, surely, than the question of action, of what to do. We have to live in this world, we have to act, we have to go to the office and do a hundred different things; and from what sort of a mind does all this action come? I can describe the background of the mind, but I think it will have very little significance if you do not relate what is being said to your own mind. Most of us think that self-knowledge is merely a matter of information, the accumulation of various explanations as to why the mind is confused; and we are easily satisfied by explanations. But really to understand oneself, one has to put away all the explanations and begin to explore one's own mind—which is to perceive directly *what is*. I must know that I am confused, that I am committed, that I have a vested interest in some system, ideology or belief, and see the significance of it; and surely, that very perception is enough in itself. But that direct perception is prevented if I am satisfied merely to explain the various causes of my confusion.

* * * * *

It seems to me that the real revolution is not economic, political, or social, but the bringing about of this new quality of the mind which is always clear. And when the mind is not clear, what matters is to perceive directly the cause of confusion without trying to do something about it. Whatever a confused mind does about its confusion, it will still be confused. I do not think we see the significance of this. All that most of us are concerned with is how to clear up our confusion, how to wipe away our darkness. But simply to perceive that the mind is confused is in itself enough. Try the experiment with yourself, and you will see. There is no answer to a confused mind, there is no way out of its confusion, because whatever way it finds, it will still be confused. Whereas, if the mind is vitally aware of, and fully attentive to its confusion, if it sees that it is muddled, that there is a distortion, that there is a vested interest—this in itself is enough. It brings about its own action, which I think is the real revolution. Because it approaches the problem negatively, such a mind acts positively. But when the mind approaches a problem positively, it acts negatively and therefore contradictorily.

New Delhi, 9th Public Talk, March 8, 1959
Collected Works, Vol. XI, pp. 201-2

Is it possible for an individual to bring about this mutation?

All change, however thoughtful, however premeditated, however desired, must still be within the limitation of time and condition. So we need a real revolution—not a mere superficial coating of color which may be called a change. We do need a deep, radical revolution in our thinking, feeling, behavior—in the way of our life. I think the more one watches oneself and the world, the more obvious that is. Superficial reformation, however necessary, is not the problem, is not the solution to our difficulties, because reformation is still a conditional reaction and is not total action. By "total action," I mean: an action out of time—not within the limits of time. So there is only one possibility and that is a complete revolution, a complete mutation.

Is it possible for an individual to bring about this mutation? Obviously, the mutation is not in the physical, not in the superficial, not in the exterior—that is impossible—but it is a mutation in consciousness. I wonder what consciousness means to each one of you. Sirs, if I may most respectfully suggest: do not just accept words and live on words. We have done that—or at least you have done that—for centuries, and look where you are! But could you examine each word that has a connotation, like *consciousness,* and find out yourself what it means, not translate it in terms of what some teacher has said? You have to feel it out, to examine and to discover for yourself the borders of consciousness, the borders of your thinking, the borders of your feeling, how far and how deeply tradition goes, and how far experience shapes your conduct. The whole of this framework of conduct, of thought, of feeling, of tradition, of memories, of racial inheritance, of the innumerable experiences that one has or a family has, the tradition of the family, the tradition of the race—all that is consciousness.

Is it possible to break this and bring about a mutation? That is the real question, which should be urgent and important to most of us because the world is in an awful mess—not only the world but also our own lives. If one is satisfied with mere reformation, then that is all right; but if one wants to go more deeply, one must inquire into the question of change and of mutation, and see that change by thought, by persuasion, by compulsion, by a process of gradual adjustment, or by the influence of propaganda surely is no change at all. Therefore, unless there is action without motive, mutation without motive, it is not change at all. I think we should be very clear on this point.

Madras, 3rd Public Talk, November 29, 1961
Collected Works, Vol. XII, p. 288

Is it possible to put an end to time?

So what do we mean by time, if there is such a thing as time? And is it possible to put an end to time? We are used to thinking in terms of a gradual process: I will change, I will be good, I should be, I must not be, and so on. All that involves time. That is: I will, in the future, do it. The very action of "will" is time. Please look at it very carefully. The action of "should" and "should not" is time, because

122

there is an interval between *what is* and what should be, and to arrive at what should be involves time. Chronologically, there is time involved when you have to get from here to your house. And equally, when you want to change *what is*, you think of it in terms of time— which is, "I should do that." Therefore the "should" implies time— which is, after gathering experience, having learned, I act. It is not learning and acting. I will go into it. Perhaps it is not clear to you for the moment... One has to explain this very carefully and go into it step by step; and your mind must be equally alert and aware, and follow the implications, otherwise you will miss it.

* * * * *

As we said, unless we understand this question of time, mutation becomes meaningless. Then we are only concerned with self-improvement, with becoming better, nobler, more kind, less kind, this or that—which involves time. So, we see that where there is the function of knowledge as will, time is involved. And when time is involved between the actor and the action, there are other factors coming into being, therefore the action is never complete. I intend to give up something—that is, I will do it tomorrow. What is taking place between now and tomorrow? There is an interval, a lag of time. In that space, there are other factors coming in, other pressures, other strains. Therefore what should be is modified already, and so is my action. So the action is never complete. I start out to do something tomorrow, inwardly—give up, do, conform, imitate, and so on—and there are other factors, other pressures, other strains, other circumstances that come and interfere; therefore there is always, between *what is* and what should be, the action which is being modified all the time, and therefore such action is never complete.

Madras, 4th Public Talk, January 2, 1966
Collected Works, Vol. XVI, pp. 21-2

The altogetherness of time is the active present. A verb is in its essence the active present, is it not? The verb "to be" includes "has been," "being," and "will be"—that which was, that which is, and that which is to be. But most of us are concerned with the progression of what has been, through *what is*, to what will be. That is our life, and we are functioning, acting in those terms: the past flowering in, and being modified by the present, thereby creating the future. Our action, which is already determined by yesterday, is modified by today and shapes what will be tomorrow. In other words, for most of us the cause and the effect are separated by an interval, a gap in which the cause inexorably becomes the effect, and which by Indians is generally called *karma*.

Now, if you examine very closely this chain of cause and effect, you will find that our action is not so completely dependent on the original cause, but may arise from something entirely different. That is, a mango seed will always produce a mango tree, never a palm or a tamarind. The cause is fixed in the very nature of the mango seed, and it produces a fixed effect. It cannot do otherwise than produce a mango tree. But with us the situation is quite different, because what was an effect becomes a cause, which is constantly being modified in the present through various influences, and may therefore produce an effect entirely different from the original cause. So with human beings the cause is never fixed, it is always undergoing a change, and that change is reflected in future action. The understanding of this fact is the total comprehension of action.

New Delhi, 7th Public Talk, March 6, 1960
Collected Works, Vol. XI, p. 364

There is only one total action—which is to die, dying.

There is only one action that is total; that is death. Right? There is no argument, no intellectual quibbling about death. There is no opinion, you do not cite your religious books, you cannot escape from it, you cannot avoid it. You do not ask death, "Give me another day." So there is only one total action—which is to die, dying.

Now dying, for most people, is negation; dying is like suicide! And because we have not comprehended the extraordinary nature of death, we—the clever, the intellectual people—make life into something that has no meaning at all. Life, then, has no meaning any more. Has your life any meaning any more? Please, sirs, do look at it! Has your life any meaning—going to the office, earning a livelihood, supporting a family, having sexual pleasures, driving in a big car or in a little car, or walking? What does it all mean to you—writing a book or not writing a book, doing some petty little social reform, belonging to some little society, and all the rest of it? What does it all mean? And the more you question living, the torture of it, the less meaning it has. And all the clever people write useless, meaningless books; out of despair they write about philosophy, they invent a philosophy. But we are not talking of a suicide, we are not talking of a despair as the ultimate action. We are pointing out that death is the only action which is total and complete—like love. Love is also total action. Love has no contradiction. But our love is hedged about with jealousy, with anxiety, with loneliness; it is "my love" against "your love," "my family" against "your family," "my nation," "my tribe" against "your tribe," the "south" against the "north." And we say we love; [but] our love is a contradiction.

So we have to understand death. And it is only in the understanding of death that you will know what love is. Or if you understand the whole nature of this contradiction, which exists as pleasure, then you will understand the total action of love, because love and death go together. You have to understand this extraordinary mystery of death.

Rajghat, Banaras, 3rd Public Talk, November 28, 1965
Collected Works, Vol. XV, p. 345

Does the state of inquiry exist when there is a positive approach, or only when there is a negative approach?

Now how does one inquire? Do please pay a little attention. What is the way of inquiry? How does one set about it? Does the state of inquiry exist when there is a positive approach, or only when there is a negative approach? By a positive approach I mean looking at the problem with a desire to find an answer. When I am frustrated, in despair, and I want to find an answer, there is a motive for my exploration, is there not? My search is the result of my desire to find a way out. So I will find a way out, but it will be very shallow and empty. I will rely on some authority, or follow a system, which will give me despair again tomorrow. Being unhappy, miserable, sorrow-laden, in a state of incessant conflict, I want to escape from this whole business; so there is a motive, and this motive creates a positive action; and such positive action, which is search with the demand for an answer, is very limited; it does not open the door to the heavens.

Bombay, 7th Public Talk, January 13, 1960
Collected Works, Vol. XI, pp. 291-2

Motive is the positive...When you have done an act without motive, then you will know about the negative.

Saanen, 3rd Public Dialogue, August 6, 1965
Collected Works, Vol. XV, p. 264

...knowing that the whole of your life, from the moment you are born to the moment you die, is conforming, imitating, obeying, adjusting to social laws or to a particular idiosyncrasy which is your own particular character; when you are faced with that, you realize that any activity born of thought, born of an idea, born of a concept—as an idea, an ideology, a formula, a tradition, or a prompting from the past—is imitative.

Then what is one to do? I hope I have made my question clear. Our brain says, "You must act, you must do something when you are confronted with this immense, very complex problem." Your reaction, the reaction of the brain, is to do; it is to think, to find a way out. Now, to find a way out, to do something about it, is what we call positive action. That is what we always do. I lack courage and I must find a way to overcome it; and so I develop various characteristics which I call "courage to face fear." That is our operation always. When we are confronted with a problem of any kind, the instinct, in reply, is to do something about it, either through thought, through emotion, through action, or through some kind of activity—which is the activity of the old brain. Right? The old brain is the result of time, experience, knowledge of the past; therefore it is imitative, and its response to a problem will inevitably be imitative.

So what is one to do? We said that the response of the old brain is imitative and whatever it does has no answer. And that response of the past is what we call "the positive activity" of life—which only breeds more confusion, more conflict. So you are confronted with this immense question: that the old brain is imitative and its responses are imitative; therefore thought, in which is included the feeling and the emotion and all the rest of it, is imitative; and therefore through thought you cannot find a way out. The intellect is not the door through which you can escape from the past, nor is emotion. Therefore all positive action must entirely cease—which means the old brain must be completely negative, which means the old brain must be completely quiet. You are following? The old brain can only be quiet if it has observed its activity in the light of its own perception.

Madras, 3rd Public Talk, December 29, 1965
Collected Works, Vol. XVI, p. 18

...merely to cultivate or to think about the "action which is devoid of reaction" is another form of reaction. Therefore we must approach the question of action which is extraordinarily positive, only negatively.

New Delhi, 5th Public Talk, January 18, 1961
Collected Works, Vol. XII, pp. 26-7

The mind must surely be in a state of complete uncertainty—that means, in a state of complete inaction, of not knowing; a mind which is not saying, "I know," "I have experience," "It is so." A mind which says, "I know" is incapable of solving any complex problem of living, because life is moving, because life is not stagnant.

Poona, India, 2nd Public Talk, January 25, 1953
Collected Works, Vol. VII, p. 150

Questioner: ...If we do as you say, we become unable to function in professional life.

KRISHNAMURTI: No, sir. The gentleman says that in professional life all action is within the field of the known. Of course! It must be! Otherwise you couldn't act as a doctor, as a scientist, as a professional.

That's simple. But when that field of action enters into the psychological field and tries to solve human problems, then no problem can be solved. Sir, to remain a technician without the psyche using that technology, that knowledge for its own purposes—you might write a book, but if you say, consciously or unconsciously, "I'm writing a book because it gives me power, position, prestige," then it becomes a poison, then you cease to be a writer; you want fame. It is all very simple when once you understand all this.

Paris, 3rd Public Talk, May 22,1966
Collected Works, Vol. XVI, p. 180

Having inquired, analyzed, having wandered around, tried all the positive ways, followed the various paths, and not having found any answer, your mind is now completely in a state of negation. It is not waiting for an answer, not hoping, not expecting that someone will tell you. Isn't that right? Please don't agree—for God's sake, don't agree! Now, when your mind is in that state of complete negation, you can approach anew all your problems, and then you will find that they can be resolved totally and completely, because it is the mind itself that has been creating the problem. The mind has been treating each problem as a separate, fragmentary issue, hoping thereby to resolve it. But when the mind is completely quiet, negatively aware, it has no problems at all. Don't think problems won't arise—it is inevitable; but as problems arise, the mind can deal with them immediately. Do you understand?

Saanen, 5th Public Talk, July 20, 1965
Collected Works, Vol. XV, p. 213

Can I face a fact without interpreting it? If I separate the fact from me, if I am lonely, I am the observer and the loneliness is the thing observed. Then the actor comes into being, the actor being me. I can do something about it. I can replace it, cut it out, suppress it, resist it, justify it, struggle against it, run away from it, adjust myself to it, deny it or rationalize it, but if I see that anger is me, that loneliness is me—the rationalizer, the thinker, the actor—if I see that the observer is the observed, then there is no experience, then action becomes impossible in the ways I am used to as action.

128

When this takes place, contradiction and effort cease. If there is no contradiction, there is no effort. This doesn't mean that my mind is asleep. In the very effort to get rid of my dependence, my anger, my passion, my lust, in that very process of conflict the mind is breaking itself up. Conflict in any form, at any level, physical or psychological, breeds further conflict, and therefore the organism as well as the psyche is wearing itself out.

Action with regard to the fact of emptiness is not possible. The observer now is the observed, and action with regard to any fact doesn't exist. From that arises the negation of action. Inaction is the most tremendous action. The positive action that we know is reaction. The observer denies the fact. He denies that the fact belongs to him, and therefore he can act. When the observer is the observed, which is the fact, action becomes impossible. The mind which has previously divided itself into the observer and the observed has no division. There is no conflict between the observer and the observed. When this takes place, there is silence. In silence there is tremendous attention.

* * * * *

Silence takes place in total inaction, which is positive action. Silence is emptiness.

Rome, 5th Public Discussion, April 14, 1966
Collected Works, Vol. XVI, pp. 121-3

The observer has always acted as though the observed is something different from himself; then he could act. But when he realizes that the observer is the observed, all action ceases on his part, and therefore all effort; and therefore there is no fear at all.

This requires a great deal of inward inquiry, inward observation, step by step without coming to any conclusion. Therefore the mind must be extraordinarily alert and sensitive and swift. And when there is no fear—because the observer is the thing which he has externalized as fear, which he is himself—then there is no longer this action which was positive, that is, doing something about fear. Then the observer is the observed. In that state there is complete inaction; and that complete inaction is the highest form of action.

So there is no effort at all. It is only the dull mind, the mind that's committed, the mind that is "achieving-not achieving," that is in constant battle, struggle; [it is only that mind] that makes an effort; and this effort, the struggle, is considered the positive way of life. It is the most mischievous way of life. And in this total inaction, when the observer realizes that he is the observed, then in that total inaction there is an action which is not of effort. Let's leave it there for the moment. I hope you understand some of it.

Ojai, 4th Public Talk, November 6, 1966
Collected Works, Vol. XVII, pp. 72-3

IX.
In Summation

Because everything is falling to pieces around us, there must be an action of a totally different kind, an action not according to anybody, not even according to the speaker. We are going to find out for ourselves what is action, how to live—because living is action.

This is the last talk of this year. I think the more one observes the world's condition, the more clear it becomes that there must be a totally different kind of action. One sees in the world, including in India, the confusion, the great sorrow, the misery, the starvation, the general decline. One is aware of it, one knows it from reading newspapers, magazines, and books. But it remains on the intellectual level, because we do not seem to be able to do anything about it. Human beings are in despair; there is great sorrow in themselves, and frustration; and there is the chaos about one. The more you observe and go into it—not intellectually, not verbally, but actually discuss, observe, act, inquire, examine—the more you see how confused human beings are. They are lost. And there are those who think they are not lost because they belong to a particular group, a circle. The more they practice, the more they do certain things, the more they do social work, this or that, the more they are sure that the world is going to be changed by their particular little act.

The world is at war, and you think that by a particular prayer, a few of us—people gathered together and speaking certain words—can solve this enormous question which has remained unsolved for over five thousand years; and you keep on repeating them, though knowing that war can never be stopped that way. So each one belongs to a certain group, to a certain political party, to a religious sect, and so on, and remains in it more and more, holding on to the past, to what has been; and one is caught in it. One admits, when it is pointed out, that there is chaos, general decline, deterioration, outwardly and inwardly;

and one realizes that man is lost. And without finding out why he is lost, why there is so much chaos and misery, without examining, without going into it very deeply, we answer superficially, saying that we are not following God, or we do not love; we give superficial, platitudinous answers that have no value at all.

And during these talks, if one has listened to them at all, one must have come to the question: Why this mess, why this confusion? If you inquire very deeply, you will find that man is lazy. The chaos is brought about through man's laziness, indifference, sluggishness, because he accepts. That is the easiest way to live—to accept; to adjust to the environment, to the conditions, to the culture in which he lives—just to accept. This acceptance breeds dreadful laziness. It is very important to understand that we, as human beings, are very lazy. We think we have solved the problem of living by a belief, by saying, "I believe in this or that." That belief is essentially based on fear and therefore the incapacity to solve that problem of fear—which indicates deep-rooted laziness.

Please observe yourself. You fall into a pattern of thought and action, and there you remain, as that is the easiest way—you don't have to think; you have thought a little bit about it, perhaps, but now you do not have to think. You are that; you are carried along by outward events, or by the push of your own little group. That gives you a great deal of satisfaction, and you think you are doing extraordinarily good work; and you dare not question because that is very disturbing. You dare not question your religion, your community, your belief, the social structure, nationalism, war; but you accept. Please look into yourself. You are so lazy. This chaos is due to this laziness because you have ceased to question, ceased to doubt—because you accept.

Being conscious of this terrible mess that is going on outwardly and inwardly, we expect some outward event to bring about order; or we hope that some leader, a guru, this or that will help us out—that way we have been living centuries upon centuries, looking to somebody else to solve our problems. To follow another is the essence of indolence. Somebody comes along; he has probably thought out a little bit and had one or two visions; he can do this or that; and he tells you what to do, and you are quite satisfied. What we really want in this world is satisfaction, comfort; and we want somebody to tell us what to do—which all indicate this deep-rooted laziness; we do not want to think out our problems, to look at them, to wipe out all the difficulties. This indolence prevents us not only from questioning, inquiring, and examining, but from dealing with a much deeper issue, which is: to find out what is action. The world is in chaos; we are in misery. All the solutions, the doctrines, the beliefs, the meditative circus that goes on in the name of meditation—none of these has solved a thing. And if we could find out for ourselves what is action, we have to act, to do something vital, energetic, forceful, to bring about a different mind, a different quality of existence.

* * * * *

One has to find out the way of life, how to live—not the method; if you have a method, a system, a practice, you have already encouraged this innate indolence. So one has to have a very sharp mind not to be caught in this trap of indolence which one is too willing to fall into.

Please listen to what is being said. How do you listen? When you listen, you listen to find out what the speaker is trying to say—to find out, not to oppose or agree. To find out for yourself means to listen, to inquire, to examine—not accepting, not saying, "I hope he will come to my point of view which is right." One has to listen, and apparently that is one of the most difficult things to do. Most of us like to talk, like to express ourselves because we have so many opinions, ideas, which are not our own; they are somebody else's. We have accepted a lot of slogans, platitudes; we trot them out and think we have understood life. So you are listening—not to explanation, not to your own prejudices, idiosyncrasies, not to what you know already, but listening to find out.

To find out, your mind must be fairly quiet. As we said the other day, to learn about anything, two states are essential: a quiet mind and attention. That is the only way you listen to another—it does not matter if it is to your wife, to your children, to your boss, to the crows, or to the call of a bird. There must be quietness, there must be attention; and in that state you are listening. That means you are already active; you are no longer sluggish; you have already broken away from this habit of half-listening, half-agreeing, half-being serious, and therefore never penetrating deeply. So, if you would listen, listen not only to the speaker but to the noise of the world, listen to the cry of the human heart, listen to the chaos, listen to your own misery, the uncertainty, the cry of despair. If you knew how to listen, then you would solve the problem. When you listen to your agony, if you have any—and most human beings have agony—you will find the answer, you will be out of it. But you cannot listen to it if you say, "The answer must be according to my pleasure, according to my desire"—then you are not listening to it; you are only listening to the promptings of your own desire and pleasure.

Here, for this evening at least, please listen to find out. Because we are going into something which requires a great deal of attention, quiet inquiry, hesitant examination—not "tell me what to do, and I will do it." Because everything is falling to pieces around us, and there must be an action of a totally different kind, an action not according to anybody, not even according to the speaker. We are going to find out for ourselves what is action, how to live—because living is action.

We have made our living so chaotic, so miserable, so immature. And to find out what is action, there must be a great deal of maturity—not in terms of time, not maturing like a fruit on a tree, taking six months. If you take six months to mature, you have already sown the seeds of misery, you have already planted hate and violence, which lead to war. So you have to mature immediately, and you will if you are capable of listening and therefore learning. Learning is not an additive process. Learning and adding, which becomes knowledge, and from that knowledge acting—that is what we do. We have experiences, beliefs, thoughts; and these experiences, thoughts, ideas have become knowledge; and on that stored knowledge we act; and therefore there is no learning at all. We are just adding, adding, adding. We have added to ourselves enormous knowledge for two million years, and yet we are at war, we hate; there is never a moment of peace, tranquillity; there is no ending of sorrow. Knowledge is necessary in the field of technology, in the field of skill. But if you have knowledge which is idea, and if from that idea you act, you have already ceased to learn. So maturity is not in terms of time and evolution, but maturity comes when there is this act of learning. It is only a mature mind that can listen, that can be very attentive and be quiet. It is the immature mind that believes, that says, "This is right and that is wrong," and pursues something illogically.

So we are going to learn together about action. You are going to think, listen. We are going to do that together, because it is your life. It is not my life; it is your life, your misery, your confusion. You have to find out what is action.

What is action? To act, to do. All action is relationship. There is no isolated action. Action, as we know now, is the relationship of "doing" with "the idea." Surely, the idea and the doing of that idea—that is excellent in the field of skill and technology; but it becomes an impediment to learn about relationship. Relationship is constantly changing. Your wife or your husband is never the same. But laziness, the desire for comfort and security, says, "I know her or him, she or he is that way," and therefore you have fixed the poor woman or man. Therefore your relationship is according to an image, or according to an idea; and from that image or idea of relationship springs action. Please give your attention to this. That is all we know as action: "I believe, I have principles; this is right, that is wrong; this should be"— and we act according to that. Man is violent; that violence is shown in ambition, competition, a brutal expression of aggressiveness—which are all the responses of the animal—and in the so-called discipline, which is suppression, and all the rest of it; and from that we act. And so there is always conflict in action.

We say that action must conform to a pattern, right and wrong, according to principles, beliefs, the tradition, the environmental influence, and the culture in which one is brought up. So action, as far as we see, as far as our life is, is according to a particular image, a particular pattern, a particular formula. And that formula, that image, or that idea has not solved a thing in the world—politically, religiously, or economically—it has solved nothing. It has not solved any of our deep, human problems. And yet we keep on insisting that is the only way to act. We say, "How can we act without thinking, without having an idea, without following, day after day, a certain routine?" So we accept conflict as the way of life—conflict which is the result of our action, of our life, of our relationship, of our ideas, of our thoughts. You cannot dispute this fact: having an idea, a principle, a belief that you are a Hindu, and so on—according to that tradition, in that framework, you live and act; and when you do that, there is bound to be conflict. The idea, the 'what should be', is different from the fact, the *what is*. That is simple. That is the way we have lived for millennia. Now, is there another way—a way of life which is action, which is relationship, but which is without conflict, which means without idea?

Listen to this. First see the problem. The word *problem*—what does it mean? It is a challenge. All challenges become problems because we do not know how to respond. Here is a problem—which is the world problem—something that is thrown at you, and you do not know any other way to respond to that problem except the old way; that is, conformity, imitativeness, repetition, establishing a habit; and from that repetitive, imitative, habitual way of life, you act. That habitual way of life is what you call "action," and that has brought about untold misery and chaos in the human mind and heart.

So that is obvious. We can proceed from that. Don't say that it is not so, afterwards. Don't pretend to yourself that it is not a fact. If you analyze it, if you go into yourself very deeply, it can be very simply put: you have a pleasure, and you want the repetition of that pleasure—sexual or any other form of pleasure—and you keep on living with that pleasure, either in memory or in thought; and that pleasure, that thought, pushes you to an action; and in that action there is conflict, there is pain, there is misery; the habit has been established, and from that habit you act.

So is there another totally different way of living, which is action? That means you have listened very carefully and attentively to the way you have lived, and you know all the implications, not just patches of it. To listen totally implies that you see, you hear the whole of the problem, not just one or two sketches of that problem. When you listen to those crows in the sense that your mind is quiet, attentive, not interpreting, not condemning, not resisting, you are listening totally. You are listening to the total sound—not of a crow, but to the total sound. And in the same way, if you can listen to the total problem of action with which you are very familiar, if you can listen totally to the problem, to the issue, to the way you live—that is, from idea there is action—then you have the energy to listen to something else. But if you have not listened totally to the present way of action, then you have not the energy to follow what is going to come.

After all, to find out anything you must have energy, and you need a great deal of energy to inquire into something totally new. And to have that energy, you must have listened to the old pattern of life, neither condemning nor approving. You must have listened to it totally—which means you have understood it, you have understood the futility of living that way. When you have listened to the futility of it, you are already out of it. Then you have—not intellectually but deeply—felt the uselessness of living that way and have listened to it completely, totally; then you have the energy to inquire. If you have not the energy, you cannot inquire. That is, when you deny that which has brought about this misery, this conflict—which we have gone into—that denial, that very negation of it is positive action.

I am going to go into that a little bit. We said, "Is there any other action in which there is no conflict, which is not a repetitive activity, a repetitive form of pleasure?" To find that out we must go into the question: What is love? Don't get sentimental, emotional, or devotional! We are going to inquire. Love is always negative—it must be. Love is not thought. Love is never contradictory—but thought is. Thought, which is a response of memory based on the animal instincts—that is, the machinery of thinking—is always contradictory. And when there is an action born of thought, that action which is contradictory brings conflict and misery. And in inquiring, in examining if there is any other activity which is not fraught with pain, with anxiety, with conflict, you must be in a state of negation. Do you understand? To inquire, to examine, you must be in a state of negation; otherwise, you cannot examine. You must be in a state of not-knowing; otherwise, how can you examine?

The way of life to which we are accustomed is what is called a positive way because you can feel it out, you can do it, day after day, repetitively, based on imitation, habit, following, obeying, being drilled by society or by yourself. All that is positive activity, in which there is conflict and miscry. Please listen to all this. And when you deny that, the very process of denying, the very process of turning your back on it is a state of negation because you do not know what comes next. Surely it is not complicated. Intellectually, it sounds complicated; but it is not. When you turn your back on something, you have finished with it.

Now, we say that love is total negation. We don't know what it means. We don't know what love means. We know what pleasure is—pleasure, which we mistake for love. Where there is love, there is no pleasure. Pleasure is the result of thought—obviously. I look at something beautiful; thought comes in and begins to think about it; it creates an image. Please watch it in yourself. And that image gives you a great deal of pleasure over that scene, over that feeling; and thought gives to that pleasure sustenance and continuity. And in family life, that is what you call love; but, that has nothing to do whatever with love. You are only concerned with pleasure; and where there is pursuit of pleasure, there is imitative continuity in time—please listen to all this—whereas love has no continuity because love is not pleasure. And to understand what love is, to be in that state, there must be the negation of the positive. Right? Shall we go on with this?

Sirs, look! When you say you love somebody—your wife, your husband, your children—what is involved in it? Strip it of all words, of all sentiments, emotionalism, and look at it factually. What is involved in it when you say, "I love my wife, my husband, my chil-

137

dren"? Essentially it is pleasure and security. We are not being cynical. These are facts. If you really loved your wife and your children—loved, not had the pleasure which you derive by belonging to a family, a narrow little group, sexually, and by furthering your own particular egotism—you would have a different kind of education; you would not want your son to be concerned only with technological studies; you would not help your son only to pass some stupid, little examination and get a job; but you would educate him to understand the whole process of living—not just one part, a segment, a fragment of this vast life. If you really loved your son, there would be no war; you would see to it. That means you would have no nationality, no separative religions, no castes—all that nonsense would go.

So, thought cannot under any circumstances bring about a state of love. Thought can only understand what is positive, not what is negative. That is, how can you, through thought, find out what love is? You cannot. You cannot cultivate love. You cannot say, "I practice, day after day, being generous, kind, tender, gentle, thinking about others"—that does not create love; that is still positive action by thought. So it is only when there is the absence of thinking that you can understand what it is to be negative—not through thought. Thought can only create a pattern and according to that pattern or formula act, and hence there is conflict. And to find out a way of living in which there is no conflict at all, at any time, you must understand this love which is total negation.

Sirs, how can you love, how can there be love, when there is self-centered activity, either of righteousness or smug respectability, or of ambition, greed, envy, competition—which are all positive processes of thought? How can you love? You can't because it is impossible. You can pretend, you can use the word love, you can be very emotional, sentimental, you can be very loyal—but that has nothing whatsoever to do with love. To understand what it is, you have to understand this positive thing called "thinking." And so out of this negation, which is called love, there is action which is the most positive because it does not create conflict, because, after all, that is what we want in this world: to live in a world where there is no conflict, where there is actually peace, both outward and inward. You must have peace; otherwise, you are destroyed; it is only in peace that any goodness can flower; it is only in peace that you see beauty. If your mind is tortured, anxious, envious, if your mind is a battlefield, how can you see what is beautiful? Beauty is not thought. The thing that is created by thought is not beauty.

138

To find out an action which is not based on idea, concept, and formula, you must listen to the whole of that structure, see, understand that whole structure completely; and in the very understanding of it, you have turned away from it. Therefore, your mind then is in a state of negation, not bitterness, not cynicism, but it sees the futility of living that way; it actually sees it and ends it. When you end something, there is a beginning of the new. But we are afraid to end the old because the new we want to translate in terms of the old. You see that? If I realize that I do not really love my family—which means I am not responsible for it—then I am at liberty to chase another woman or another man, which is again the process of thinking. So thought is not the way out.

You can be very clever, erudite; but if you want to find a way of action that is totally different, that gives bliss to life, you must understand the whole machinery of thinking. And in the very understanding of what is positive—which is thought—you enter into a different dimension of action which is essentially love. That means—to inquire you must be free; otherwise, you cannot inquire, you cannot examine; and this chaos, mess in the world demands reexamination totally, not according to your terms, not according to your fancies, pleasures, idiosyncrasies, or the activities to which you have been committed. You have to think of the whole thing anew.

And the new can only be born in negation, not out of the positive assertion of what has been. And the new can only come into being when there is that total emptiness, which is real love. Then you will find out for yourself what action is in which there is no conflict at any time—and that is the rejuvenation that the mind needs. It is only when the mind has been made young through love, which is the total negation of the life of positive thought—not through sentimentality, not through devotion, not through following—that such a mind can build a new world, a new relationship. And it is only such a mind that can go beyond all limitations and enter into a totally different dimension.

And that dimension is something which no word, no thought, no experience can ever discover. It is only when you totally deny the past, which is thought, when you totally deny it every day of your life so that there is never a moment of accumulation—it is only then that you will find out for yourself a dimension which is bliss, which is not of time, which is something that lies beyond human thought.

Bombay, 6th Public Talk, March 2, 1966
Collected Works, Vol. XVI, pp. 71-7

Bibliography

The Collected Works of J. Krishnamurti, first published by Kendall/
Hunt, 1991-1992
  Vol I (1933-34) *The Art of Listening*
  Vol II (1934-35) *What Is Right Action?*
  Vol III (1936-44) *The Mirror of Relationship*
  Vol IV (1945-48) *The Observer Is the Observed*
  Vol V (1948-49) *Choiceless Awareness*
  Vol VI (1949-52) *The Origin of Conflict*
  Vol VII (1952-53) *Tradition and Creativity*
  Vol VIII (1953-55) *What Are You Seeking?*
  Vol IX (1955-56) *The Answer Is in the Problem*
  Vol X (1956-57) *A Light to Yourself*
  Vol XI (1958-60) *Crisis in Consciousness*
  Vol XII (1961) *There Is No Thinker, Only Thought*
  Vol XIII (1962-63) *A Psychological Revolution*
  Vol XIV (1963-64) *The New Mind*
  Vol XV (1964-65) *The Dignity of Living*
  Vol XVI (1965-66) *The Beauty of Death*
  Vol XVII (1966-67) *Perennial Questions*

Commentaries on Living, Series II, Quest Books, 1988

Commentaries on Living, Series III, Quest Books, 1988

The First and Last Freedom, HarperSanFrancisco, 1975

Think on These Things, HarperPerennial, 1989